# PRAISE FOR
# WRESTLING GATORS

"Aerospace engineer, family man, and now Michigan State Senator Patrick Colbeck has personally experienced and excelled in the wide variety of life's experiences it takes to govern effectively in our times. His principled solutions are just what Michigan needs to return to the fundamental foundations upon which America was built. *Wrestling Gators* articulates why Pat Colbeck has the leadership qualities, message, and Right Stuff to make Michigan a leader in America's return to greatness!"

— *Jack Lousma, Col USMC (Ret), Skylab Astronaut*

"Part must-read autobiography, part compelling call to action, Pat Colbeck's *Wrestling Gators* is a powerful DIY guide to citizen-led government reform!"

— *Catherine Engelbrecht, president of True the Vote*

"This fascinating book gives an inside look at one of Michigan's most unlikely champions of liberty and the journey from his epiphany of governmental dysfunction through his deeply felt inspiration to take on "the machine."

Hopefully, *Wrestling Gators* will serve as a clarion call for others to find the God given courage in themselves to know that they too can make a difference.

— *Dr. Chad Savage*

"The truths in *Wrestling Gators* will help readers all across the nation to Drain the Swamp. Murky Swamps will disappear in the light of truth."

— *Cindy Pugh, Minnesota Representative*

"Drain the Swamp! Is the rallying cry of our generation. If we are to survive as a nation, it simply must be done. And if I were to pick one legislator in America to jump in and 'wrestle the gators,' Patrick Colbeck would be at the top of the list; they don't come any better than this good man. I could not be happier to know he has written an instruction manual for those of us anxious to follow his courageous lead."

— *Mike Azinger, West Virginia Delegate*

# WRESTLING GATORS

*An Outsider's Guide to Draining the Swamp*

*by*

## Patrick Colbeck

# WRESTLING GATORS

Copyright © 2018 by Patrick Colbeck

Illumify Media Group
www.IllumifyMedia.com
"Write. Market. Publish. *SELL!*"

Print: 978-1-947360-13-6
eBook: 978-1-947360-14-3

# DEDICATION

To God

You lift us up when others tear us down.

You provide us with friends when enemies rise up.

You provide an open window when others shut a door.

You meet all of our needs during our times of wants.

You love us as individuals worthy of white robes even when we are clad in tattered rags.

You speak hope into our lives when others promote despair.

You make all things possible when the world only sees the impossible.

In all matters You are faithful, and Your promises are true.

You are truly worthy of all praise and honor.

# CONTENTS

# FOREWORD

I have been a personal friend and professional colleague of the Honorable Senator Patrick Colbeck for the last eight years and have worked on a number of legislative and community initiatives including the preservation of the Michigan Traditional Marriage Amendment and Michigan's historical Right-to-Work legislation. Both efforts were and are essential to the perpetuation of our nation's constitutional republic and the restoration of freedoms lost in the recent insurgence of the secular progressive's agenda.

Pat Colbeck not only possesses the vision and foresight for our nation's return to the core principles of the Constitution and Bill of Rights, he also understands how to move from precept in theory to application in legislation and mobilization in voter participation to codify initiatives essential in reducing government expansion, hence government and taxpayer waste. His leadership on the issue of Right-to-Work is unparalleled and nothing less than a political, legislative miracle. As a result of this transformational achievement, Michigan's economy has added over a half million new jobs in a multiplicity of sectors, restoring Michigan as a leader in our nation's economic recovery and twenty-first-century prosperity. How such a remarkable political, legislative feat was achieved is of paramount importance to our nation's future and its citizens' freedom. The inspiration behind Pat's vision is crucial, as well as the *citizen assets* who helped organize the successful campaign to make personal freedom to choose a priority through Right-to-Work legislation.

In conclusion, this publication will serve as a model and roadmap to all who will dare challenge a magnanimous system of government that has grown out of control. There is obviously much work to be done, but *Wrestling Gators* is a rare record of events in history that prove no challenge is too great when the aim is to save our freedom, liberty, and union.

*BISHOP IRA COMBS, JR., D.D., a religious leader who served as a director of President George W. Bush's national and Michigan Faith-Based Initiative and currently serves as a recently appointed commissioner on the Michigan Civil Rights Commission*

# PROLOGUE

Did you ever hear the story of Jesus, the bystander, a tight rope and a wheelbarrow?[1]

It goes something like this:

There was a man who would get up early each and every day to watch Jesus walk on a tightrope strung over Niagara Falls. Each day, the man would get up early and watch Jesus get up on that tight rope and walk across to the other side without fail. One day, before getting up on the tight rope, he walked over to the man who had been watching Him faithfully day after day.

"Do you think that I could walk across the tight rope strung across the falls?" Jesus asked.

The man responded, "Yes, I have seen you do it every day for quite some time."

Jesus looked over at a nearby wheelbarrow. "Do you think that I could walk across the tight rope strung across the falls while pushing that wheelbarrow?"

The man looked over at the wheelbarrow, then looked at Jesus and replied, "Well, I've never seen you do that before, but you are the Son of God. Sure. I believe that you could do that."

Jesus simply said, "Get into the wheelbarrow."

This book is the story of my wife, Angie, and I getting into the wheelbarrow.

# INTRODUCTION

Swamps can be murky places filled with all sorts of nasty creatures such as alligators which can make life miserable and sometimes quite dangerous. This seems like a pretty good description of today's political environment in Washington, DC. President Ronald Reagan was among the first politicians to refer to government bureaucracy as a "Swamp." President Donald Trump made draining the swamp a key tenet of his presidential campaign.

Why does the swamp metaphor resonate with so many Americans? The reasons are many fold. One reason is that many of us did not fully embrace the importance of a good civics education while in school. While I have since immersed myself in a diligent study of our founding documents, I was guilty of this oversight for the first forty-three years of my life. If one is unaware of how our system of government is intended to work, it is quite natural to see the halls of government as murky enclaves. Knowledge is a great way to navigate this murkiness.

Just because you may know how to navigate the Swamp, however, does not mean that the Swamp won't make you miserable or pose significant dangers. The Swamp metaphor even resonates with those of us who do take civics seriously because we can't help but be confused as to why very few elected officials are actually serving in a manner that honors their constitutional oaths or even their own campaign literature. Something happens to many elected officials between the time they are first elected and when they run for their first re-election. It is as if they get infected by a virus carried by the swarming denizens of the Swamp. It can afflict even the best-intentioned elected officials.

The swamp metaphor also resonates with many Americans who feel shut out of the governance process. This is quite concerning for a system of government in which all powers are supposed to be delegated to the government by "We the People." People are integral to our system of government. If the majority of our people feel oppressed, shut out or ignored, we have a serious problem with our government.

Regrettably, Swamps are not limited to Washington, DC. We have swamps in many of our state capitols as well. After a successful career as an aerospace engineer, management consultant, and small business owner, I ventured into public service to restore some semblance of common sense to the halls of Lansing. I have served as a state senator for the citizens of the Seventh Senate District in Michigan for the past eight years. As someone who never served in the Michigan House or any other elected capacity besides church council, it has been a challenging experience.

After eight years serving in the state senate my drive to drain the swamp has not diminished. To clean up the Swamp properly and effectively, at some point the effort needs to be driven from the top. That is why I am running for governor of the state of Michigan in 2018. There is only so much one senator can do.

I have found that those who know how to navigate the bayous of government are typically rather tight-lipped when it comes to providing directions to visitors. It is our visitors who should be the ones providing directions, but swamp denizens have so thoroughly distorted the trails and landmarks in our capitols that it is easy for visitors to get lost. My goal with this book is to help visitors drain the swamp so that these trails and landmarks can be recognized and followed once more.

As Former Speaker of the House Newt Gingrich once sagely opined at a health care forum at which I was invited to speak in Washington, DC, "One shouldn't be surprised if the alligators bite when you try to drain the swamp." It is my hope that this book will help you drain the swamp in a way that will keep the bite marks to a minimum. Okay, let's go wrestle some gators!

# PART 1

# PUBLIC SERVICE

# 1

# THE LOST DECADE

"In five years, you're gonna be blown away" Michigan governor Jennifer Grahholm proclaimed in the 2006 State of the State Address.

Michigan was indeed "blown away" along with many of our jobs. The years 2000-2009 are often referred to as Michigan's "Lost Decade." By the end of the decade, Michigan was the only state in the nation to have a net loss of population as our family members sought greener economic pastures in other states.[1] At the start of the Lost Decade, Michigan's eighteen electoral college votes were reduced to sixteen. During the '60s, '70s, and '80s Michigan had a peak of twenty-one votes.

Over the course of the first nine years of the new millennium, Michigan is estimated to have lost 537,471 residents to other parts of the country. These moves helped to fuel the growth in states like Georgia, South Carolina, Texas, Nevada, and Arizona.[2]

Perhaps most concerning was the fact that we were losing our youth. During the Lost Decade we lost 11.7 percent of our citizens between the ages of twenty-five and thirty-four. Our families were hit hard as a result. Upon graduation, our sons and daughters were settling in other states where they would raise their families far away from their parents. Not only would our youth be without enthusiastic grandparent babysitters, grandparents would grow old with no one to look after them. My family was personally impacted by this trend. In fact, it wasn't long after graduating from the University of Michigan in 1988 that I moved to Alabama and later to Florida to find employment in the Aerospace industry. My sister and her family also moved out of state to find employment. My brother-in-law and his family moved out of state to find employment. Even when Angie and I moved back to Michigan in 1995, I spent most of my time on the road engaged in consulting contracts outside of Michigan.

Why were we losing family members to other states? The Michigan economy. Michigan's economy dramatically underperformed the US average throughout the early- and mid-2000s. During the period 2000-07, for example, while real US gross domestic product grew annually, on average, at 2.5 percent, Michigan's GDP grew at just 0.2 percent. From 2008 to 2010, annual Michigan GDP contracted 2.8 percent versus the US average of 0.4 percent. Per capita income actually dropped 8.6 percent.[3]

When I took office on January 1, 2011, the Michigan unemployment rate was 10.9 percent. Michigan had 512,698 unemployed workers. Michigan had 4,178,232 employed workers.[4] At the beginning of 2011, we were ranked fiftieth out of fifty states in unemployment.[5]

The state budget did not look much better than the overall state economy. We had a structural deficit of $1.5 billion. The rainy-day fund was down to $30 million, which was enough to run the state government for just five hours. Our total liabilities were $70 billion against an annual budget on the order of $46 billion.[6]

Like most of my fellow citizens, I was oblivious to these stats. I started the Lost Decade working as a management consultant focused primarily on the automotive industry. Like many Americans, I was too busy working to pay any serious attention to what was going on in Lansing or DC. The antics of Lansing or DC frankly did not occupy my thoughts at all. But what I did know was that a lot of people in Michigan were out of work and that families were leaving our beautiful state for greener pastures in other states.

As the decade progressed, I found myself living out of a suitcase as my client base moved from Michigan to other states. While my home was still in Michigan, I was starting to see less and less of it as I piled up the frequent flyer miles and hotel rewards. It was not the kind of life that my wife and I wanted, but I kept plugging away to pay the bills hoping that things would get better soon.

While I was faithfully doing my work in service to my clients, I assumed our elected officials were working on rectifying the problem. I assumed that the people we elected to serve us were looking out for us. I assumed that they were diligently working on policies that would make Michigan a more attractive place for all of us to live, work, and play.

As I started to pay more attention to what was going on, I found that the majority of our elected officials did not have their constituents' interests as their top priority. With regrettably few exceptions, too many were focused on ladder climbing and their own job security.

The Lost Decade was not simply a time of problems, though. It was also a time of awakening. By 2009, Angie and I were awake and actively seeking what we could do to turn things around in our beloved state of Michigan and our nation as a whole.

# 2

# GOING TO NINEVEH

If you are interested in understanding why a successful aerospace engineer and small business owner would ever make the decision to go into politics, this is the chapter for you.

I often say that my decision to go to Lansing had a lot of parallels with the story of Jonah in the Bible. When the Lord told Jonah to "go to the great city of Nineveh and preach against it," because of its wickedness, "Jonah ran away from the LORD and headed for Tarshish" (Jonah 1:2-3). To put it mildly, I was about as eager to go to Lansing as Jonah was to go to Nineveh. After all, Lansing was the source of many of the policies that had driven so many of my friends and families to greener pastures in other states.

Why would I want to go to Lansing?

I'm an engineer, and the political environment isn't exactly known to be a safe haven for engineers. Engineers deal with facts and figures. Politicians deal with emotions and are typically *very* selective with facts and figures.

Growing up, I was an extreme introvert. Some of my most stressful times as a kid involved going shopping because I did not know what to say to the cashier. (Kids today don't know how easy they have it with automated cashiers.) Engineering was a natural choice of professions when I grew up. Give me a calculator, a CAD system, throw in a few complex differential equations and I'm happy as a clam at high tide.

In fact, I was quite happy applying my aerospace engineering degrees on inspirational projects such as the International Space Station for Boeing and NASA and later on a virtual reality training system for the Department of Defense. Those were good times. They were followed by a career in management consulting that included six years on my own as a small business owner. None of my clients were politicians. I had never been active in politics. In fact, I knew very little about politics except for what I heard on the news and talk radio.

Another reason going to Lansing didn't make sense is that the political environment isn't exactly known as a safe haven for Christians either. A friend once remarked to me that nothing good happens in Lansing after 7 p.m. I have found that to be true—especially when it comes to the bleary-eyed votes in favor of bad legislation.

From a worldly perspective, running for office was a fool's errand.

We had zero political experience, unless you count church council.

We had insufficient savings to shut down my consulting business and run for office.

We had limited knowledge of the lingo of Lansing known to lobbyists and veteran staffers.

Even if I were successful in my bid for a state senate seat, I would be taking a 40 percent pay cut and making decisions that would likely tick off 50 percent of my neighbors on a daily basis.

Why would anyone in their right mind want to take that kind of job?

Good question.

From a worldly perspective there is no logical answer. Prior to making the decision to run, however, I had been gradually waking up to the fact that our lives are meant for much more than this world can give.

It all started with Good News! Via de Cristo, a lay apostolic ministry designed to wake up the hands and feet of the church (i.e. parishioners and congregation members) so that they engage in the mission of the church. *Via de Cristo* means "way of Christ," and the mission of the church is to let others know about the way of Jesus. You see for ten years prior to receiving the call to run for office, I had been working on my piety, study, and apostolic action through Via de Cristo retreat weekends and reunion groups.

In short, I had been gradually tuning my radio station to Jesus.

I wasn't alone. Angie joined me in this journey along with many of my friends and family members.

You may be saying to yourself, "I thought this book was about politics. I don't want to read a book on religion." Trust me. This book is about politics. But if you really want to know what motivated me to get into politics it is critical to know about our faith journey.

One of the key milestones on this journey, believe it or not, was when we decided to get rid of cable TV. Our cable outlet was broadcasting sexually explicit material on the TV guide channel at 7 p.m., a time when many young kids would be tuning in. We felt convicted that we were financially supporting this and similar content and finally cut the cord. We replaced our cable with a

Christian internet-based TV service called Sky Angel. On Sky
Angel, we could still have access to news and old TV shows like
*Magnum P.I.*, but Higgins would be bleeped out when he used
the Lord's name in vain.

One of the content providers on the new service was an
organization called WallBuilders, which harkens back to the book
of Nehemiah. One day we saw a documentary called *America's
Godly Heritage* by David Barton of WallBuilders. It talked about
the providential history of our nation in ways we were never taught
in school, even parochial school. My inquisitive engineering
mind developed an insatiable appetite for information on our
Founding Fathers and how our government was designed to work.
I voraciously read and studied our founding documents. I even
read Michigan's constitution. That is how motivated I was, and
am to this day, to understand how our government is supposed
to work.

Did you know that at least twenty-nine of the fifty-six signers
of the Declaration of Independence had been trained in schools
whose primary purpose was the preparation of ministers? Have
you ever heard of what the British referred to as the Black Robe
Regiment? They were ministers that made the moral case for
independence from Britain and freedom. Early ministers were
not shy about asserting themselves regarding what today would
be classified as taboo political matters. Perhaps that is why there
has been a concerted movement to separate religion from politics,
starting with the Progressive Era at the turn of the last century.

Another key milestone on our journey towards serving in
elected office was on April 15, 2009. Angie and I heard about
a political rally at which my former Detroit Catholic Central
classmate, former congressman and former presidential candidate

Thaddeus McCotter, was going to speak. The event was a Tea Party Rally at Kellogg Park in Plymouth, Michigan. Angie and I dutifully constructed a crude sign which said PEOPLE ARE BROKE. THE CONSTITUTION ISN'T. We parked in a public parking lot an uncomfortable distance away from the site of the rally. This meant that we had to drag the sign awkwardly from the parking deck to the event. We tried to be inconspicuous, but I couldn't shake the feeling of discomfort as we navigated through passersby until we got to the rally. Little did we know that this "discomfort" was only the beginning. We still had no inkling that we would ever consider running for public office.

Once at the event, we felt strangely at home. We were surrounded by about eighteen hundred people. The organizers would have been happy with five hundred. What bound all of us together? The answer to this question was obvious to all who attended. We all loved our country but were increasingly frustrated by a government clearly operating outside of the bounds of its limits. We were all united by a common belief that our government should abide by the constraints specified in the Constitution and stop spending money they did not have.

We started the event in prayer. There was patriotic music from Tony and Cameron Lollio of the Skinny Raccoons. People in the crowd and on stage were talking passionately and knowledgably about the Constitution. Pastor Levon Yuille of the Abolitionist Roundtable spoke eloquently about our American Heritage. Folks held signs which read TAXED ENOUGH ALREADY or GOD ASKS FOR ONLY 10 PERCENT. There were Gadsen Flags and American Flags everywhere. Topics ranged from our Founding Fathers to a national debt that was rapidly growing out of control. We were surrounded by veterans, school teachers, pastors, off-duty police officers, moms, dads, grandparents, children, business owners, and people of all ethnic backgrounds.

The only group with meager representation was politicians. In fact, Thaddeus McCotter was the only one present at this large gathering.

It was clear to us from this event and the events to follow that many people, especially those in the media, continue to treat the Tea Party as something of an enigma. For those who are still confused, let me help.

A Tea Partier is simply someone we used to call an American.

At this gathering of Americans, we met quite a few people who would later become some of our most dear friends. Among the dearest of these friends are the Keenas. Jim Keena was one of many eloquent speakers at the event. We were in the crowd with Jim's wife, Audrey, and their exceptional kids, Ella and John. As we often do, Angie and I offered to take a photo of them together at the event. We exchanged contact information and ended up getting together later on for a high-end lunch together at a McDonald's in Northville. Since most of our friends and family were not plugged in politically at all, we found the event tremendously cathartic as we shared our observations about the political landscape with people who had the same concerns.

Not long after our fancy luncheon, we were invited by the Keenas to attend a Tea Party steering committee meeting. It was at this meeting that our friendship circle expanded significantly. In addition to the Keenas, we were introduced to Michigan's Rattle With Us Tea Party founders, Maribeth Schmidt and Sharon Lollio, as well as fellow tea partiers Andy and Deb Brandt, Maribeth's husband, Jim, Kim Richardson, and Sharon's husband, Marco. Together, we formed the nucleus of the Rattle with Us Tea Party.

This first meeting was little more than a social event where we all got to know each other a little better. At this meeting, we formed instant friendships, which we cherish to this day.

As we learned more and more about our nation's heritage and how our nation was intended to work, we became bolder in our public assertions to this effect. For example, during a meeting with the website consultant for my prospective client, Matt Dame, our technical discussion quickly developed into a political discussion. In fact, Matt swears that he was the first to suggest that I run for political office. In this light, he is at least partially responsible for much of the gray hair that I have accumulated over the past 8 years. Matt soon became a fixture of our Rattle with Us meetings where he selflessly handled all of our audio-visual needs. He and his wife, Barb, have become dear friends.

Under the leadership of Maribeth Schmidt, Sharon Lollio, and Marco Lollio, along with the selfless service of many others, Rattle with Us regularly held forums at the Plymouth Cultural Center where seventy to a hundred people attended. People were hungry for information about the issues facing our nation and our state. Members would research a topic then come and speak about the topic to the group. One of my early public speaking assignments was Obamacare. I had read all 1,017 pages of HR 3200, an early version of HR 3590 that would eventually come to be known as Obamacare. From my earliest reading, it was clear that it had more to do with control than care.

Other speakers researched the national debt and how our money was being spent. We explored topics like Agenda 21, smart meters, road construction, and Common Core Standards Initiative. We also engaged in community forums that covered topics such as office hours for our elected officials. We didn't limit our engagement to the four walls of the Plymouth Cultural Center, though.

At one forum in January of 2010 we engaged a local representative during one of his coffee hours with constituents. Angie and I had performed quite a bit of research prior to the meeting. We came loaded with information about his voting record. When we questioned the official, who was a likely candidate for the seat in which I now serve, he consistently misrepresented the facts about his record and key budget issues. I came out of that meeting incredibly frustrated by the prospect that he would likely be my representative in Lansing. It was one of those moments when you just knew that it was important to take action. I started thinking about what had previously been unthinkable—at least to me—running for office. I wasn't too thrilled about the prospect of running for office, so I began praying. I even went so far as to give God a deadline: February 21, 2010.

On the day of the deadline, my devotion was from 1 Corinthians: "Do you not know that in a race all the runners run, but only one gets the prize? Run in such a way as to get the prize" (1 Corinthians 9:24).

And that's exactly what Angie and I did.

I wore out two pairs of shoes in the process, but in the end, we defied all worldly odds and defeated four former state representatives to become the first person elected directly to the state Senate in over three decades without any previous political experience.

A stunned reporter in the wake of the election results asked me what I attributed to my success. Sharing a truth conveyed by our Pastor Brad Powell in the months leading up to the election, I simply said, "Where God guides, He provides."

He repeated the question. I repeated my answer. "Where God guides, He provides."

He still didn't believe his ears and repeated the question. I repeated my answer. "Where God guides, He provides." And that's exactly what he printed in the newspaper for all of the world to see. To this day, that article remains Angie's favorite news article covering my public service.

God truly did provide and continues to provide to this day.

That was only half the story, though.

Throughout the election, we experienced numerous mini miracles. One of the first features Via de Cristo. Typically, when a candidate announces a run for office, he takes to the media to let everyone know what a swell guy he is and why everyone should vote for him. I didn't have that opportunity. Within minutes of announcing my candidacy at a tax day Tea Party event in Kellogg Park in Plymouth, MI, I sped away to serve as the head chapel cha on a Via de Cristo weekend. The day after the retreat, I received the news that the primary front runner dropped out of the race. Where God guides, He provides.

Later in the race, the general election front runner dropped out of the race right before the filing deadline, leaving a relatively weak general election opponent for me. Where God guides, He provides.

We didn't even realize that we needed a campaign consultant. One of our fellow candidates who was running for our local state representative seat, Lori Levi, helped us out. Lori and her family are fellow members of Northridge Church. She was running for the state representative seat in our district and was much more politically savvy then we were. She introduced Angie and I to a wonderful campaign consultant named Jennifer Murray. An experienced, consummate political staffer, Jenn became a dear friend and served as my chief of staff for six years before taking on the reins of her father's consulting business. Where God guides, He provides.

During my first visit to Lansing to talk to GOP power brokers, I felt completely like a fish out of water. As I roamed the halls of the state capitol for the first time, it became clear that the grandeur of the building, the pomp of its proceedings, and the titles of its occupants were intended to impress and project an aura of authority. This aura was very intimidating to someone who simply wanted to serve and get to work helping to fix the state government. Just when I was feeling about two inches high under the majestic ceilings of the capitol, I stopped by the office of the then-former Senate majority leader, now congressman, Mike Bishop. In his office is where I first met Bobby Ray. Bobby Ray served as the receptionist for a string of Senate majority leaders for twenty-two years until Arlan Meekhof unceremoniously broke this string in 2015. At a time when I was questioning why I would ever want to serve in such a pretentious, oppressive, and dark place, Bobby truly was a ray of sunshine. She taught me that there were some true gems serving the people of Michigan in Lansing. Where God guides, He provides.

One of my most memorable meetings was with the sitting, term-limited state senator of the Seventh District, Bruce Patterson. At six foot five, Senator Patterson can be a pretty intimidating fella with his characteristic handlebar mustache. If you recall my fear of cashiers, I wasn't the most assertive individual in the world. To make matters worse, he is an exceptional lawyer who can easily make you feel like you are being cross-examined even while eating lunch. Suffice it to say, I was intimidated. Beneath the sometimes-gruff exterior, there is a heart of gold, though, and he has become a dear friend and trusted confidant. Senator Patterson provided vital fundraising guidance and connected me to many of the key leaders in our community. Where God guides, He provides.

Raising money is an intimidating facet of campaigning. It turns out that businesses are not in the habit of giving candidates free yard signs, mailers or TV ads. Who'd figure? It actually takes money, lots of money—way beyond what most people's circle of family and friends can provide—to let voters know that you are willing to serve them in public office. Angie and I did not have a personal war chest or wealthy family members to lean on to help fund the campaign. To compound matters, in order to win, I felt it was necessary to shut down my consulting business during the campaign. That meant that Angie and I would be without any income for nine months. Even if we were to receive free yard signs, mailers, and TV ads (which we didn't), we still needed to pay our mortgage, utilities, and other living expenses. In order to keep the lights on at home, we liquidated *all* of our personal savings and retirement accounts (paying a 10 percent penalty for early withdrawal). In short, we were *fully committed*. Even after liquidating all that we had, we calculated that we would still need twenty thousand dollars to help keep the lights on until I received my first paycheck as a state senator. Angie and I took to our knees. We prayed specifically for twenty thousand dollars. Within days, I received an unsolicited offer of a consulting contract for the only two-week time period without a campaign event. The contract paid twenty thousand dollars. Where God guides, He provides.

We still needed to raise money for the campaign, though. As we quickly found out, it ain't easy. As an engineer and even as a management consultant, I was not in the habit of asking people for money. One of our first fund-raisers was organized by our friends in the Rattle with Us Tea Party. They brought in Thayrone X to serve as master of ceremonies for the event. Thayrone is the host of the popular "On the Edge" radio talk show on WAAM 1600 in Ann Arbor. It was at that event that Angie and I first met Thayrone and his lovely wife, Linda. They were the first "celebrities" Angie and I ever met in person. Today, they are among our dearest friends, but at the time, we were star struck that a radio show host would spend time supporting some nobody's run for the state Senate. It just goes to show what can happen when one "gets in the wheelbarrow." Where God guides, He provides.

As further demonstration that we were fully committed, we liquidated everything of value that we thought might generate decent bids at our fund-raiser auction. That included putting up for auction my Star Trek uniform, a sentimental souvenir from my geeky engineering days with Boeing working on the International Space Station. I even auctioned off my largest remaining pieces of the Berlin Wall. I traveled to East Germany in 1990 to deliver a paper at the forty-first International Astronautics Federation conference in Dresden, East Germany. It coincided with the reunification of Germany. It was very difficult to part with the memento, but part I did. In the end, we raised twenty-seven hundred dollars at the event. Where God guides, He provides.

One of our next fundraisers featured Rick Green. Rick Green is a former state representative in Texas, TV personality, and featured speaker at WallBuilders. Because Rick tended to talk about God in his talks, we were discouraged from featuring him at a fund-raising event due to potential push back from voters. We featured him anyway. Rick wowed the attendees with the great information about our Founders that first woke us up to the need to get involved in politics. We raised another one thousand dollars and saw no discernible push back from voters. Where God guides, He provides.

Along the way, even my opponents in the primary supported me financially in the general election. Where God guides, He provides.

Money alone does not win elections. Ground troops are essential. I am happy to say that we have been blessed with strong grassroots support from citizens of all ages and backgrounds on the campaign trail. I continue to be amazed by the diversity of those who came together to help get us across the finish line. Even though I had never considered running for office until a little over six months before the 2010 primaries, it seems as though every decision that I had made up to the decision to run for office provided one of the puzzle pieces needed for victory. For example, before deciding to run, I accepted an appointment to serve on the board of the Canton Charter Academy. CCA was consistently one of the top five public schools in the state. My service as treasurer of the CCA board introduced me to a remarkable woman by the name of Diana Noble. Diana's insights as a parent of former CCA students and her selfless pursuit of the best interests of our students serve as a shining example of exceptional civil service. Diana, her husband, Rudie, their son, Brendan, and daughter, Breana, have become some of our most cherished friends to this day. We gained much more than friendship as a result of my public service on the board. Serving on the board also put me at ground zero of some of the most important issues facing education which would serve me well as a member of the Senate Education Policy Committee. Where God guides, He provides.

When I look back I can certainly see God's hand at work. My going to Detroit Catholic Central (CC) for high school not only provided me with a strong foundation of religion, morality, and knowledge, it also connected me to a network of exceptional friends and professionals that make up the CC family. My decision to go into business for myself resulted in many business connections through local Chambers of Commerce that turned into friends and supporters. When we look back upon how all of these puzzle pieces fit neatly together, we are overwhelmed at how awesome a project manager God truly is. He knew what I would need to prepare me for business and then politics. For eleven years I earned a living as a management consultant, which laid the groundwork for the freedom to run for office and the connections to make it happen. God knit together a network of family and friends that clearly exceeded by leaps and bounds what my own limited ability could accomplish. Where God guides, He provides.

There were many other mini-miracles throughout the campaign, not the least of which was the overwhelming support from voters as we won by a margin of 11 percent in my first ever campaign for office. Where God guides, He provides.

I did not want to run for office. My wife did not want me to run for office. From a worldly perspective, it was a fool's errand. Running for office was truly a matter of putting our faith in action. In other words, we were firmly in the wheelbarrow.

# 3

# HITTING THE GROUND RUNNING

In Michigan, we have term limits for state elected officials. State senators are limited to two four-year terms. State representatives are limited to three two-year terms. Governors are limited to two four-year terms. It is safe to say that all of our elected officials are relative short-timers. I think that is a good thing.

In my position I often meet enthusiastic students who are eager to get into politics. I truly appreciate their interest in civic engagement, but I consistently advise them to hold off on running for office until they have experienced the real world and how the laws truly impact their lives. There is no better way to gain an appreciation of the impacts of ever increasing taxes and fees than living under one's own roof for some time. Better yet, open a business. That's what I did. This experience has proved invaluable as I evaluate legislation before the Senate. I'm not saying that our political system is not in need of fresh perspectives. It is. I'm just saying that the world is much more complex, and it is probably impossible to get an appreciation for the how the economy works in school—even in the best of schools.

As a senior design engineer working on the Environmental Control System and Airlock for Boeing on the International

Space Station, I learned a very important adage. "Make sure that you have a solid understanding of what you are changing *from* before you change *to* something else." As you might imagine, the Space Station is fairly complex just like a state government. For my first Class I (Station-wide) Change Proposal my team and I had proposed consolidating all of the oxygen/nitrogen systems aboard the Space Station into a single $O_2/N_2$ system resulting in significant cost savings. (It seems like I've always been an advocate of cutting costs while improving services.) I soon learned, however, that the change, while providing savings, impacted much more than I anticipated. It impacted laboratory operations, airlock operations, and logistic operations. The change impacted the physical location of equipment in all of the pressurized modules as well as the exterior truss. In order to implement the change effectively, much work needed to be done. Until we started processing the change request, I did not have a true appreciation for how complex the physical layout and station operations really were.

I know what some of you may be thinking. Doesn't this analogy support the need for a "professional class" of elected officials who truly understand how the system operates? The answer is no. The purpose of government as expressed in our Declaration of Independence is simply to secure the rights of the governed. It is *not* the purpose of government to run the lives (i.e., operations) of its citizens. The best qualifications of elected officials should be a sufficient understanding of "real life" to best understand how the laws used to secure the citizens' rights impacts their daily lives. Lawmakers need to have real-world experience living under the laws they pass. The broader the experience the better.

Opponents of term limits often point to the long time it takes many legislators to spin-up on the issues and understand how government works. Why is our government so complicated that it takes years to spin-up on?

The US Constitution fits into a shirt breast pocket. If we were governing in accordance with the principles found in that document, government would be limited and its operations would not be difficult to digest. The fact of the matter is that government should not be complicated. It should not require a "professional class" to interpret and guide its operation. After all, our laws are meant to be followed. To be followed, we need to understand how to follow them.

What opponents of term limits (mostly lobbyists and legislators) are *really* saying is that they are tired of investing time in developing new relationships. Businesses prefer large clients to small clients for similar reasons. The cost of sales is much lower. Make no mistake, it is all about sales for most lobbyists.

According to conventional political wisdom, I had no business serving in the Senate. After all, I was an experienced engineer and management consultant, not a political science major or lawyer. No one in my family ever talked about politics, much less ran for office. Our family had always been focused on sports, work, and church. Furthermore, since I had never run for any other elected office, I had "not paid my dues."

Rest assured, though, as an elected official, I studied up on how our government is supposed to operate. As I alluded to before, I studied the US Constitution and the Michigan Constitution, to which I swore an oath to support. I studied Senate procedures. I studied the Senate Republican Caucus rules to the extent that they were defined. I even attended a Legislative Leadership

Forum that serves as the orientation for new legislators. Being that it was my first elected office, I was one of only two senators amidst a classroom full of state representatives. The other state senator was attending as a refresher course being that he had been out of office for quite some time prior to being elected as a state senator. I went on to study the issues as well. All the studying and orientation proved invaluable and continues to be valuable to this day. I will readily cede the enormous value of institutional knowledge in the development of good public policy. We need to make sure, however, that institutional knowledge does not supersede the experiences of those who live under the auspices of public policy.

Invariably, the solutions proposed by policy "experts" are to increase the size of government and increase taxes. These solutions invariably benefit those in government or those dependent upon government funding. I am happy to say that I was not alone in my concern about the preponderance of "tax first" solutions. Many other freshmen legislators, including some Democrats, thought the solutions offered are rather narrow. But successful public policy all too often is not driven by the merit of the policy, it is driven by relationships. That observation put me at a disadvantage from the start. It wasn't that I wasn't able to get along with others. It was that most of my fellow senators had already served with one another for six years in the State House before I showed up on the scene. This is basic team dynamics 101. The new guy is typically the odd man out, but there are exceptions to the rule.

One of the first major doors that opened occurred at my first formal meeting of what would become known as our Senate Republican Caucus. During this meeting, the members of the caucus were to elect our leadership team. I explain this process in a bit more detail later in this book, but suffice it to say it is a key step in the selection of a Senate majority leader. The meeting was held quickly after the results of the election were finalized. Overall there were ten leadership positions to be filled in a caucus of twenty-six Republican senators. I didn't realize how important this post-election election was.

The meeting started with the nomination of the Senate majority leader. Once nominations were closed, all of the members cast their vote for Senator Randy Richardville. The meeting then proceeded with the nomination and election to the remaining nine leadership positions. When it came to the nomination of the assistant caucus chair, there was silence. As it turns out, the assistant caucus chair was the lowest rung on the leadership team totem pole. No one had been lobbying for this position prior to the meeting. I broke the silence by asking what the position entailed. In a nutshell, my colleagues shared that the position was basically that of a glorified meeting facilitator for caucus meetings. As a management consultant for over eleven years, I was a frequent meeting facilitator so I nominated myself. Senator Pappageorge quickly made a motion to close all nominations. The next thing I knew, I was a freshman legislator serving on the Senate leadership team.

As an engineer, I was trained to solve problems. We have many problems in government. In fact, I often say that serving in government is like being an auto mechanic who opens the hood of a customer's car every morning only to find yet another wire that is not connected properly. This means that I have had plenty of opportunities to apply my problem-solving skills. Later, I will share many of the solutions to the problems that I have worked on during my tenure in the Michigan Senate. It is my hope that these solutions will be of use to other legislators in Michigan as well as in other states.

The chapter on how government really operates is intended to help lower the slope of the learning curve for most candidates willing to get into the wheelbarrow.

# 4

# STAYING THE COURSE

Shortly after being elected, Sharon Lollio approached me with an important question. "Now that you are elected, how are you going to keep from becoming part of the problem rather than part of the solution?"

It got me to thinking about how best to stay on course. I sat down and developed what I referred to as the "Compass." The principles outlined in the Compass (See Figure 1 on page 47) were taken from my campaign literature. It was also worded to align with objectives that I supported in the plans of other influential leaders such as Governor Snyder and the objectives of groups such as the Business Leaders of Michigan and the Michigan House of Representatives. Right from the start, I attempted to focus on what we all had in common.

On the back of the card are the following quotes from famous American leaders.

> "Of all the dispositions and habits which lead to political prosperity, religion and morality are indispensable supports. In vain would that man claim the tribute of patriotism, who should labor to subvert these great pillars

of human happiness, these firmest props of the duties of men and citizens. The mere politician, equally with the pious man, ought to respect and to cherish them."

*— George Washington*

"Government's view of the economy could be summed up in a few short phrases: If it moves, tax it. If it keeps moving, regulate it. And if it stops moving, subsidize it."

*— Ronald Reagan*

"No government ever voluntarily reduces itself in size. Government programs, once launched, never disappear. Actually, a government bureau is the nearest thing to eternal life we'll ever see on this earth!"

*— Ronald Reagan*

"It will be of little avail to the people, that the laws are made by men of their own choice, if the laws be so voluminous that they cannot be read, or so incoherent that they cannot be understood: if they be repealed or revised before they are promulg[at]ed, or undergo such incessant changes, that no man who knows what the law is to-day, can guess what it will be to-morrow."

*— James Madison*

"It would reduce the whole instrument to a single phrase, that of instituting a Congress with power to do whatever would be for the good of the U.S. and as they would be the sole judges of the good or evil, it would be also a power to do whatever evil they pleased. It is an established rule of construction, where a phrase will bear either of two meanings, to give it that which will allow some meaning to the other parts of the instrument, and not that which would render all the others useless. Certainly no such universal power was meant to be given them. It was intended to lace them up straitly within the enumerated powers, and those without which, as means, these powers could not be be carried into effect."

*— Thomas Jefferson*

"The same prudence which in private life would forbid our paying our own money for unexplained projects, forbids it in the dispensation of the public moneys."

*— Thomas Jefferson*

"They who can give up essential liberty to obtain a little temporary safety deserve neither liberty nor safety"

*— Ben Franklin*

"Sell not virtue to purchase wealth, nor liberty to purchase power"

*— Ben Franklin*

"A little neglect may breed mischief; for want of a nail the shoe is lost; for want of the shoe the horse is lost; for want of a horse the rider is lost; for want of a rider the battle was lost."

*— Ben Franklin*

"The philosophy of the school room in one generation will be the philosophy of government in the next."

*— Abraham Lincoln*

"No man is good enough to govern another man without that other's consent."

*— Abraham Lincoln*

"History is not history unless it is the truth."

*— Abraham Lincoln*

"The Constitution is not an instrument for the government to restrain the people. It is an instrument for the people to restrain the government – lest it come to dominate our lives and interests."

*— Patrick Henry*

I carry a copy of the Compass in the vest pocket of my suit. This Compass also sits on my Senate floor desk right next to a Bible gifted to me by my brother-in-law, Ed Martin, his wife, Joan, and daughter, Emily. This Bible was signed by Rev. Franklin

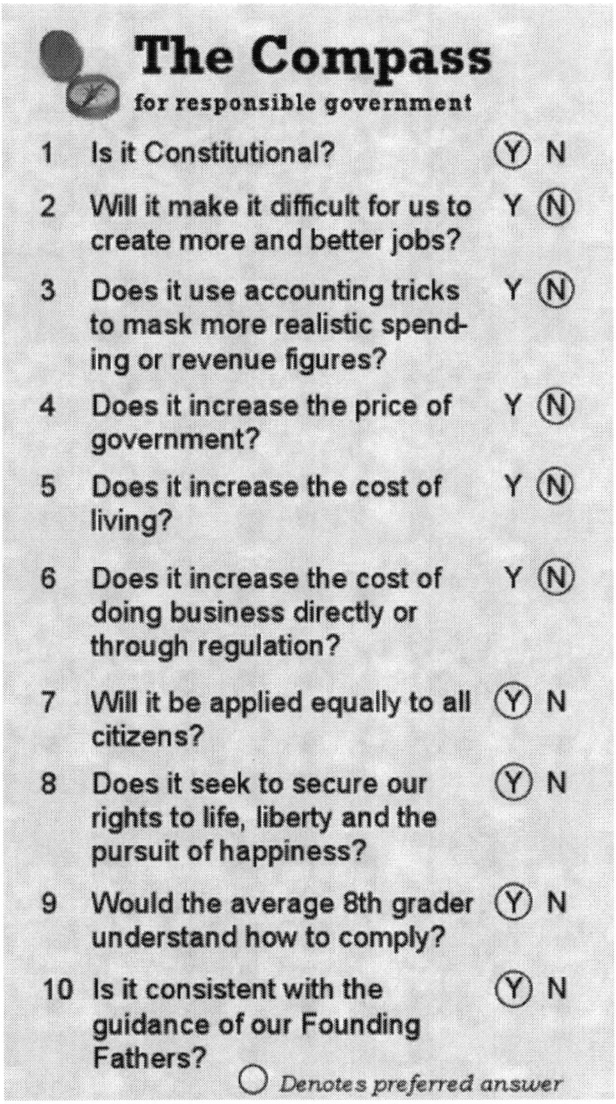

## The Compass
for responsible government

1  Is it Constitutional?                                  (Y) N

2  Will it make it difficult for us to    Y (N)
   create more and better jobs?

3  Does it use accounting tricks        Y (N)
   to mask more realistic spend-
   ing or revenue figures?

4  Does it increase the price of        Y (N)
   government?

5  Does it increase the cost of         Y (N)
   living?

6  Does it increase the cost of         Y (N)
   doing business directly or
   through regulation?

7  Will it be applied equally to all    (Y) N
   citizens?

8  Does it seek to secure our           (Y) N
   rights to life, liberty and the
   pursuit of happiness?

9  Would the average 8th grader         (Y) N
   understand how to comply?

10 Is it consistent with the            (Y) N
   guidance of our Founding
   Fathers?
                    ◯ Denotes preferred answer

*Figure 1 Voting Compass*

Graham referencing Romans 1:16 which reads, "I am not ashamed of the gospel, because it is the power of God for the salvation of everyone who believes: first for the Jew, then for the Gentile".

I use this voting compass to guide my decisions when it comes to complicated pieces of legislation. Furthermore, I provided copies of this compass to lobbyists and other legislators to indicate how I would vote on a given piece of legislation.

Some people find this approach to governance too rigid. Lobbyists in particular prefer elected officials who are "malleable." I can be very malleable on a bill's language, but I am not malleable on principles. After all, I ran for office on a set of principles. I pledged to follow those principles once elected to office. Most of my constituents appreciate this perspective.

Principled service does not preclude collaboration. This is a fallacy that some disingenuously promote. As an engineer, the creative process of design often started with the customer specifying a set of requirements. For the purpose of this illustration, please think of these requirements as principles. Much more often than not, one would find that there are many different designs that would satisfy the same set of requirements. Engineers would then collaborate with other members of the design team, including the customer, to identify the design that *best* satisfies the requirements. Typically, the evaluation of these designs would be captured in what is often referred to as an engineering trade study. In a trade study, each design is scored against each of the customer requirements. The design which scores the best is the design which is implemented. When I was an instructor at SpaceCamp in Hunstville, Alabama, I used the design of an astronaut's living compartment as a means of instructing students in how to execute an engineering trade study. It is not a difficult process.

If rolled out wisely, I believe that the concept of a Voting Compass could be a game changer in the legislature. If it were to gain traction within both branches of the legislature, it would effectively neuter the influence of special interests and ensure that legislation is guided by principle not politics-as-usual.

Unfortunately, this systematic, principled approach to policy and budget development is not often adhered to in the halls of government. The preferred design method appears to be a "throw it against the wall and see if it sticks" approach. It is the equivalent of designing a plane without analyzing its lift and drag, building the plane, getting some brave soul to see if it will fly, and going back to the drawing board if it crashes.

We can save both elected officials and those whom we serve much heartache if we would simply agree upon basic principles before designing any legislation.

That's what our Founders did. They first agreed upon a set of principles that would guide the governance of their new nation. These principles are found in the Declaration of Independence. These principles opened the door to the definition of the Articles of Confederation and later the Constitution. Principles preceded legislation.

The principles of the various political parties sometimes clash. When this happens, it is important to pursue the best interests of those who elected you. Some clashes need to be engaged. Principled service paints with bold colors not pale pastels. In the next chapter, we will discuss one of the boldest colored challenges faced by our state during my tenure in the Michigan Senate: Right to Work.

# 5

# HOW MICHIGAN
# BECAME A RIGHT-TO-WORK STATE

On December 12, 2012, Governor Rick Snyder signed SB 116 into law making Michigan the twenty-fourth Right-to-Work (RTW) state in the United States of America.[1]

The following morning, Rush Limbaugh said in his morning update: "Michigan Republicans: way to go! You've got political courage and onions!"

I believe it is fair to say that the passage of RTW in Michigan answered the call of President Reagan for bold colors.

One of the reasons Right to Work required such bold colors is that the term "Right to Work" is a misnomer. We all have a right to work. In the absence of Right-to-Work legislation, though, workers would be forced to financially contribute to a union as a condition of employment regardless of how well that union represented their best interests. I prefer to call it "Workers Choice" as it simply provides rank and file union members with a choice as to whether or not to financially contribute to a union or not.

The passage of RTW in Michigan was indeed a shock to many political pundits. It has had national implications. After all,

Michigan is the de facto home of the labor movement. The United Auto Workers (UAW) union was formed in Michigan. Big labor is the principle funding stream of the progressive movement. The tide of progressivism has been waging war against constitutional principles such as the freedom of assembly ever since the turn of the twentieth century. The passage of RTW in Michigan stemmed that tide. Joe Lehman, president of Michigan's nonpartisan research institute Mackinac Center said, "This is not a Michigan Victory but a national victory. Do we have any problems at the federal level that look harder than bringing right-to-work to Michigan?"[2]

Since the 2012 passage of RTW in Michigan, my friends in Wisconsin, West Virginia, Missouri, and Kentucky have also passed this legislation prompting serious discussions in DC about passing a national RTW law. The road to passage of Right to Work in Michigan probably deserves a book of its own to do it justice, but I will try to give a brief overview in the next few pages.

Less than a year before this legislation passed, political pundits were telling me that it would be decades before Michigan could possibly become a RTW state. We were not convinced. After all, Michigan had a Republican governor, a super majority in the Senate (26 of 38 seats), and a majority in the House (64 of 110 seats). If not then, when?

For me, the road to giving Michigan workers a choice as to whether or not they must pay union dues started while knocking on doors. Even though I had been a union member when I worked for $3.60 an hour as a stock boy at G&W Discount Drugs and I had headed up the newly formed Program Management Department of AAR Cargo Systems, which was a union shop, I had never heard of the term Right to Work until I knocked on the door of a home with a truck in the driveway proudly sporting a UAW sticker on its bumper. After I introduced myself to the gentleman who answered the door, the first question out of his mouth was "Do you support Right to Work?" I asked him what Right to Work was. After he described it to me, I said that if it provided more freedom to workers, I was in favor of it. He proceeded to ask me if I had a yard sign he could put on his front lawn. That was an easy Yes.

When I returned home after a long day on the doors, I proceeded to do further research on Right-to-Work laws. I came to appreciate it as a way to restore the First Amendment right to freedom of assembly. I later came to appreciate it as the key to job growth in our state and stemming the exodus of workers from our state, but the drivers behind my initial pursuit of the law were pretty simple. I saw it as my job to pursue legislation that preserved constitutional principles and satisfy a sensible policy request from a constituent.

When I started my service in the Senate, I found that I was not alone in my desire to pass RTW. In fact, the vast majority of my colleagues supported its passage. There is a difference, however, between supporting an initiative like RTW and leading the passage of RTW. As the last remaining Republican state senator from Wayne County, the ancestral home of the UAW, I was an unlikely leader of this effort. Usually, major policy initiatives were led by legislators from so-called safe districts featuring strong majorities of likeminded voters. The Seventh Senate District was not a "safe district," but it featured something much more important: residents impacted first hand by the job drain resulting from forced unionization policies. It was clear to even this political newbie, however, that the passage of RTW would not be easy even with the support of my colleagues and disaffected members of the rank-and-file, blue-collar workforce.

In support of this effort, I reached out to a kindred spirit in the other chamber, then-State Representative Mike Shirkey. Both of us were freshman legislators who apparently didn't know any better than to take on this challenge. We did have the sense to know, however, that we couldn't do it alone.

Together, we sought the advice and counsel of RTW policy experts such as Gary Glenn (now a state representative), the Mackinac Center, and National Right to Work. We began to assemble a grassroots army featuring organizations such as the Michigan Freedom to Work Coalition, Americans for Prosperity, and Union Conservatives. The Mackinac Center team received excellent support from Paul Kersey, Patrick Wright and later Vinnie Vernuccio. The National Right to Work team led by Mark Mix featured invaluable support from Don Loos. The Michigan Freedom to Work Coalition was blessed with tireless advocates led by Norm Hughes, Tim Austin, Tim Bos, Steve Franz, Glen Frobel, Jerry Allen, and Randy Bishop. Our ever-present Americans for Prosperity team was led by Scott Hagerstrom, Annie Patnaude, Chris McCoy, and Louie Cascerelli.

One of the most remarkable grassroots organizations that joined us in the RTW fight was Union Conservatives, founded by a rank and file union worker, my good friend Terry Bowman. Terry was joined by Brian Pannebecker in courageously promoting RTW as an active union member. Terry, Brian, and other union members like them deserve special recognition. They were very vocal in their promotion of RTW *while* holding union jobs on the assembly line. Needless to say, every day at work for them was an "adventure." Despite these "adventures," every night they would be out making the case for workers to have their freedom of assembly restored by the passage of RTW. These two and others like them are the true heroes in the passage of RTW.

With the grassroots army assembled, we got to work refining the case for passing the legislation. That was the easy part since Michigan was tired of losing population and jobs in the wake of the Lost Decade. Indiana, our neighbor to the South, had passed RTW in early 2012 threatening to siphon more jobs from Michigan. At the time, the top 5 job-growth states over the past decade were Right-to-Work states. The bottom 5 job-growth states were in non-Right-to-work states. Michigan was fiftieth in 2010.[3] Per capita personal income in two-thirds of the RTW states is higher than non-RTW states.[4] Prior to the passage of Right to Work, 17 percent of the Michigan's workforce were forced to be in a union. Once it passed, 17 percent of Michigan workforce would still be in a union—*if* they chose to be in a union.[5]

I took the lead on drafting the legislation and routing it for legal review. We had ten different versions of the legislation ready for whatever policy avenue would be available. By the time our legislation was introduced, it had gone through numerous high-powered legal reviews to make sure that we had the i's dotted and t's crossed in preparation of the inevitable legal battles that would ensue upon passage. In addition to the draft legislation, I prepared a strategy PowerPoint, a business case flyer, and a 285 task plan in Microsoft Project to guide our deliberations.

In order to succeed in making Michigan a Right to Work state, it became evident that we would need more than ground support. We also needed a higher echelon of political influence that I referred to as "air support" that would be able to open up the ears of leadership and provide the resources necessary to defend the legislation once it passed. Our "air traffic controller" was Ambassador Ron Weiser.

The first step towards getting this air support was to convince our air assets that we had the votes. To this end, Mike whipped his House colleagues. I whipped my colleagues in the Senate.

Mike was blessed to have the support of leadership in the House, namely Speaker Jase Bolger. In the Senate, Senate Majority Leader Randy Richardville openly oppposed my efforts to pass Right to Work. As a freshman legislator, I had to proceed very carefully.

Borrowing the tactics that Senator Richardville used while running for Senate Majority Leader, I discretely drafted and circulated a sign-up sheet with the words "In order to form a more perfect union" across the top followed by a list of principles which I was asking my colleagues to support. Many were reticent to lend their name to the document but said they were supportive regardless. I assured them that the list would be kept confidential. It has been kept confidential to this day. Once we had seventeen names on this list, it was clear that we were in striking distance of the twenty votes needed in the Senate. These seventeen commitments triggered our air traffic controller to launch the senior official lobbying effort needed to get the remaining three votes.

Gradually and with much relentless positive action, we were able to paint the Senate majority leader and our hesitant governor into a corner that left only one option: support the legislation. It was not easy.

Right to Work invokes quite a bit of emotion. It evokes anger from folks who have been deceived. It evokes anger from those who have been doing the deceiving, after all, they depend upon the forced flow of union dues to fund their lifestyles. If rank-and-file members were actually able to withold their union dues if they felt that their best interests were not being served by their union, that would upset the carefully nurtured quality of life of the union bosses. In RTW states, union bosses have to work hard to earn the support of the rank and file. We were taking on the union bosses.

Right to Work also evokes fear. Quite a bit of fear. Lawmakers are fearful because they know that the union bosses will organize protests that often go beyond a vocal redress of grievances. Legislative leadership is fearful because RTW has more often than not resulted in embarassing failures that threaten majorities in future elections. The "air assets" or policy power brokers are fearful because of the large amount of money that would need to be raised and subsequently put at risk in order to defend the law and support lawmakers who had the courage to support the law.

I must admit that I was fairly slow to realize the depth of emotion involved in this issue. I merely focused on the fact that it was the right thing to do if we were serious about providing our citizens with good jobs and stemming the exodus from our state. It wasn't until I noticed evidence that my home phone had been tapped that I fully realized how RTW was not a run-of-the-mill piece of legislation. This was the big leagues. One day when I came home from work, I noticed that one of the utility panels on the side of my home was open. Upon closer examination, I noticed that it was the panel for our phone line. Dangling in the breeze were two wires. I brought in a professional investigators to examine the box, and it appeared that there had recently been some listening device connected between the wires, which had been removed. Chilling.

I often joke with my wife that whoever had installed the device probably removed it after listening in on a few too many phone calls of us saying, "I love you, Shnookums." The fact of the matter is, though, that they probably removed it once they realized that we no longer used our land line.

Through it all we pushed fear to the wayside and remained focus on why we were pursuing the legislation. In fact, I coined the term Phil 4:8 strategy to demonstrate how our approach differed from that of others when passing contentious legislation. This strategy focused upon the value proposition for our citizens in passing RTW. We highlighted how the current forced unionization policy was at the heart of Michigan's Lost Decade. As divisive as the union bosses would make the issue, it was even more divisive to continue policies that divided up Michigan families in light of the population exodus from our state. We focused upon why RTW was the best policy for our state as a whole and kept promoting that message. Typically, proponents of contentious legislation take what I refer to as a "whack a mole" approach. Any time someone pops up in opposition, they proceed to whack them into submission either by public humiliation or behind the scenes politicking. Is it any wonder why previous attempts to pass RTW failed?

By fall of 2011 our Phil 4:8 wheels were in motion. All we needed now was a miracle. In order to expedite this miracle, our grassroots army turned up the heat. One of the pressure points was the following editorial that I penned for news outlets in October of 2011:

### "Right to work" is about getting people "back to work"

There are some people claiming that now is not the right time to pursue right to work in Michigan. However, it is important to note that "right to work" is about getting people "back to work." We cannot say "not now" to folks who are unemployed. We need a sense of urgency in our pursuit to get Michigan back to work.

This past year, under the leadership of our Governor Rick Snyder, Michigan has taken great strides to improve the job growth environment in our state, but we all agree that there are significant reforms that still need to be adopted. In the Senate, we have outlined a job growth policy featuring significant tax and regulatory reforms along with investments in infrastructure. These are all important initiatives that will spur job growth. We still need to do more, though, to make Michigan #1 in job growth.

An examination of the policies in states with significant job growth reveals that one of the largest remaining obstacles in Michigan to job growth is forced unionization. The case for labor freedom is compelling. The top five job growth states from 1999 to 2009 are right to work states. The bottom five over that same period are non-right to work states including Michigan, which ranks 50th in job growth. Over that same time period, real personal income grew twice as fast in right to work states than non-right to work states and the per capita personal income in 2/3 of the right to work states is higher than in Michigan. In addition, the last 10 new auto manufacturing plants have been built in right to work states.

I know that there are folks who are attempting to paint a different picture, but the positive impact of "right to work" where it has been implemented is undeniable. Rather than get engaged in a match of statistician Ping-Pong, though, I simply ask you to ask yourself the following questions: Where are your kids going to find work once they graduate? Where are your grandkids going? Where are your neighbors moving? Odds are that your answers feature right to work states.

This begs the question...why haven't we pursued right to work in Michigan? The answer, quite simply, is "fear." For years, we have avoided a substantive discussion on labor freedom because there are those who fear "a divisive confrontation." Meanwhile, we continue to lose jobs and break up families as our youth seek better fortunes in other states.

It doesn't have to be a divisive confrontation. The truth is that labor freedom is not anti-union. On the contrary, it promises to strengthen unions by making union management more accountable to the members that they represent. One could make the case that the status quo featuring forced unionization is anti-union. In 1999, Michigan had 963,000 union jobs. Today, we only have 627,000 union jobs. Union rank and file members are among those pushing for labor freedom as a means of making unions more responsive to their views.

Currently, 17% of Michigan's workforce is unionized. When labor freedom legislation is passed, the fact is that we will still have 17% of Michigan's workforce in unions – if union management is responsive to the needs of their members. As we grow jobs in Michigan, the fact is that we will grow more union jobs – if union management is responsive to the needs of their members.

I am a staunch supporter of the right of individuals to join a union, but I will also vigorously defend the rights of individuals who do not wish to join a union. This is America…the land of the free and home of the brave. It is time to restore our commitment to the principles that made our country the most prosperous country in the history of the world. It is time to commit ourselves to labor freedom."

The grassroots army that we had built provided additional pressure points by distributing flyers, hosting forums, submitting editorials, and encouraging lawmakers to swallow their courage pill.

This pressure produced results. Bob King, president of the UAW, flinched. In so doing, he provided the miracle we were looking for in the form of a massive policy overreach known as Ballot Proposal 2. Ballot Proposal 2 would have essentially created a fourth branch of government by establishing that collective bargaining agreements superceded any laws passed by the legislature. Opponents to forced unionization such as myself fought against this proposal with the truth. We took to the streets and to the paper, including this editorial I wrote:

> The 2012 election will feature a total of six ballot proposals. Proposal 1 is a referendum on the Emergency Manager Law. Proposals 2 thru 6 would result in amendments to our Michigan Constitution if passed. Before you vote on any of these proposals, I encourage you to understand exactly what you are voting for or against. You may be surprised to know that the proposal language that appears on your ballot is NOT the language that will be enacted into law. The language on the ballot is simply a collection of marketing talking points. You need to view the ACTUAL petition language to see exactly what law would be enacted. The easiest way to see the actual language as well as get a TRULY non-partisan perspective on the impacts of the proposal is to go to the Ballot Issues page at the Citizens Research Council of Michigan website (www. crcmich.org).
>
> One of the most concerning ballot proposals is Proposal 2. Per the ACTUAL petition language, the passage of Proposal 2 would nullify all "existing or future law" enacted by state legislators or local municipalities dealing with the subject of collective bargaining. In court proceedings, the proponents of the proposal refused to list the impacts of its passage. "Attorney Andrew Nickelhoff, representing the Protect Our Jobs Coalition, said he did not know how many laws would be changed, and argued that it's not the

coalition's responsibility to spell out all of the details on the petition or in the ballot language" (Source: M-Live, August 22, 2012). I would contend that the so-called "Protect Our Jobs" Coalition does have a very good understanding of which laws would be changed. They just don't want the voters to know, especially since the passage of the proposal would adversely impact many of the workers whom they advertise are being protected by this proposal.

Active members of police and firefighting unions would likely not be supportive of the nullification of PA 312 of 1969 which guarantees binding arbitration for public safety officers. Retirees would likely not be very thrilled by the nullification of PA 12 of 2012 which ensures that retired Detroit Police and Firefighters would have representation on the board responsible for the management of their pension. They would also likely have heartache with pending legislation like SB 1189 which would require equal treatment of retiree board members and active workforce board members. Please note that many of these reforms are bi-partisan public acts. For example, PA 12 of 2012 was sponsored by Representative Durhal (D) and SB 1189 was sponsored by Senator Mark Jansen (R).

You should also know that taxpayers would likely see a minimum $1.6 Billion tax increase to pay for collect bargaining agreements devoid of requirements for public employees to contribute up to 20% towards their healthcare premiums and receive fair retirement benefits on par with private sector employees. Numerous other legislative reforms that many rank and file members as well as citizens-at-large appreciate such as prioritizing teacher performance over longevity, criminal background checks for school employees and school bus safety rules would be subject to nullification with the passage of Proposal 2.

Clearly, not all of your interests are protected by collective bargaining representatives alone. If that were the case, the aforementioned bills would not have been necessary. Now the responsibility to protect your rights as public safety professionals, retirees, and taxpayers passes from your elected state representatives to you. I strongly urge that you review the ACTUAL wording of proposals such as Proposal 2 before casting your vote. If you don't like a statute passed by the legislature, you can always vote in representatives that will pass a better law. Once you vote to change our constitution, however, your changes will be there for a very long time.for good or for bad."

The UAW proposal was clearly an overreach to all objective observers. It was deceptively called the Protect Our Jobs proposal. The only jobs it would have protected, after all union jobs in the state disappeared, were those of union bosses not willing to serve the best interests of their rank-and-file members.

On November 6, 2012, Proposal 2 was dutifully rejected with a 15 percent margin by 57 percent of voters. This resounding defeat provided the necessary encouragement to colleagues, including our governor, who were on the fence. They now agreed we should pursue passage.

On December 6, the Michigan Senate voted 22-16 in favor of legislation that would give private sector workers the freedom to choose whether or not to financially support a union. Even the once recalcitrant Senate majority leader voted in favor of the legislation. On the the same day, the House voted 58-52 in favor of legislation to provide this choice to public sector workers. Each chamber's legislation than went over to the other chamber for consideration.

On December 11, the House voted in favor of the private sector legislation and the Senate voted in favor of the public sector legislation. That same day, Governor Rick Snyder signed the bill into law. Per our Constitution, in order for Immediate Effect to be granted on legislation, two-thirds of both chambers must agree. We did not have sufficient votes to obtain Immediate Effect for the legislation in the House so the effective date of the law was March 31, 2013.

In the wake of the RTW passage, I was honored to have received the Senator Paul Fannin Statesman of the Year Award from Mark Mix at a NRTW event in Memphis, Tennessee, but I readily acknowledge that the passage of RTW in Michigan never would have happened without what I refer to as a tightly knit patchwork of supporters. Every component was needed for us to be successful. We needed both ground cover and air cover as I like to say.

Four plus years after the enactment of this law, Michigan is on the rebound. Our unemployment rate has risen from the bottom of the pack to the middle of the pack. Our per capita income growth is the fourth fastest in the nation. And best of all, our state is growing as families no longer need to be split up to find work in other states.

Why was it so difficult to pass Right to Work with Republicans in control of each decision-making body? Chapter 8, How Government Really Works, provides some insights in this regard. In the meantime, suffice it to say that there is often a significant difference in believing that something is right and having the courage (or blissful ignorance) to do the right thing.

# 6

# PROTECTING OUR RIGHTS

At its core, Right to Work is simply about protecting one of our First Amendment rights—the freedom of assembly. According to the Declaration of Independence, the purpose of government is to "secure the rights of the governed." I have found that if we do not exercise our rights—or worse yet, not even know they exist—we will lose them. This is why I routinely follow in the footsteps of my good friend from WallBuilders, Rick Green, and ask students and scouts to which I am privileged to speak to name the five freedoms guaranteed in our First Amendment. When they stall on listing them, I gently point out that if they can't name them, they will lose them.

The first ten amendments to the United States Constitution are referred to as the Bill of Rights. The authors of our Constitution did not believe that the Bill of Rights was necessary since the government constructed under the Constitution already enumerated limited powers. If the Constitution did not say that they government had a power, they didn't have it. Technically, they are absolutely right. Unfortunately, nature truly does abhor a vacuum. The anti-federalists, led by George Mason, knew that we needed explicit prohibitions against the infringement of individual rights or government would gradually usurp these rights. Sadly, time has proven them to be right. Even sadder, however, is that even with these rights being explicitly listed in the Bill of Rights, our government continues to infringe upon them. As it turns out, liberal (in the original sense of the word) activist Wendell Phillips was proven most right when he observed, "eternal vigilance is the price of liberty."

It is in the spirit of Mr. Phillip's sage observation that I have found myself called to promote policies and statutes that secure our liberties. Many times these efforts fall under the blanket of social issues. Most legislators shy away from tackling social issues. Because they often deal with issues of religion and morality, discussions surrounding these topics are often much more contentious then arguments over fiscal matters such as budget appropriations or economic development policies. Just because they may be contentious, however, does not mean that we should forgo engaging in a defense of these rights.

In any discussion of our rights, it is important to first understand where our rights come from. Our Declaration of Independence clearly delineates the source of our rights as our Creator. "We hold these truths to be self-evident, that all men are created equal, that they are endowed by their Creator with certain unalienable Rights, that among these are Life, Liberty and the pursuit of Happiness." Clearly, our Founders were not afraid of social issues.

It is important to note that the Right to Life is the first right delineated. Without the Right to Life, none of our other rights matter. In this light, is it any wonder that I am staunchly pro-life? I have introduced or co-sponsored numerous bills to protect the most vulnerable among us – the baby in the womb.

Liberty is the next unalienable right to be listed. A unique appreciation for this right is what makes America truly exceptional among all of the other nations of the world. "It is for freedom that Christ set us free" (Galatians 5:1). Around the world, liberty is synonymous with America. This is why America has an immigration problem not an emigration problem. God has imprinted a passion for freedom in the hearts of mankind and America is the only nation in the world founded on an appreciation of this truth.

The right to the pursuit of happiness is why we have such a term as the American Dream. With the underpinnings of the rights to life and liberty, Americans are enabled to pursue their own unique, individual dreams. It makes us a land of opportunity not oppression.

Many of our Founders were apprehensive about the erosion of our unalienable rights over time. In fact, many of them refused to ratify our US Constitution without an assurance that it would be supplemented by an explicit list of rights. In response to these concerns, the first ten amendments to the Constitution called the Bill of Rights were added.

Our First Amendment rights in particular are actively targeted in today's culture. Let's start with our first liberty, the freedom of religion. Today, many seek to convert this pro-faith protection into an anti-faith right or a freedom *from* religion. Such a conversion from the Judeo-Christian roots of our founding would effectively establish secularism as our national religion. As John Adams once wisely opined, "Our Constitution was made only for a moral and religious People. It is wholly inadequate to the government of any other." If we were to remove this pillar of our society, we would systematically erode all of our other rights because under the social compact of our founding, these rights come from God. This is why I am such an adamant defender of religious liberty. In addition to introducing legislation to protect the voices of religious leaders, I have also consistently stepped in to defend every day citizens who have been persecuted for their religious beliefs. If we do not assert our freedoms in this manner, we will lose them.[1]

Next in the crosshairs is our First Amendment right for the freedom of speech. One only has to review the speech codes on many of our college campuses to realize that there are many seeking to convert this freedom into a freedom *from* speech. They use trigger warnings, free speech zones, and speaker bans to curtail speech. Our First Amendment is not necessary to protect us from speech that we like. I have sponsored free speech legislation to promote civil dialogue on campuses and penalize those who infringe upon free speech rather than those seeking to exercise their right.

We already talked about how forced unionization laws infringe upon freedom of assembly, but there are many other examples of the infringement of this right. In fact, Michigan election law singles out religious leaders for prohibitions that deny their freedom of religion, freedom of speech, *and* freedom of assembly. Religious leaders who express "religious disapproval" on the basis of the political views held by members of their congregation can be fined $500 and/or jailed for ninety days. Religious leaders are the only members of tax exempt organizations prohibited from such actions under Michigan election law. I have introduced legislation to remove these provisions from the law.

Even the freedom of the press is under attack. CBS reporter Sheryll Atkinson discovered evidence that her computer had been hacked with keystroke logging software. In January 2015, she testified before the Senate Judiciary Committee where she alleged that the FBI and other government agents were responsible for this hacking, which gave them the ability to read all of her communications with sources and even the ability to delete information on her computer.

As an elected official who conducts regular office hours, values constituent communications with my office, and encourages social media interactions with those of differing opinions, I can assure you that the freedom to petition the government for redress of grievances is alive and well. Having said that, it is also where one can observe the coarsening of society first hand. Being open to a redress of grievances does not mean that a legislator should be subject to defamation of character or threats of violence.

Let's move on to the Second Amendment. Our rights continue to be infringed upon despite the clear text of the Second Amendment, which states that "the right of the people to keep and bear Arms, shall not be infringed." The Michigan constitution is even clearer. It states that "every person has a right to keep and bear arms for the defense of himself and the state." Yet in Michigan, we have Gun Free Zones analogous to the Free Speech Zones on our college campuses. In other words, we now have the right to keep and bear arms as long as we don't work in a school or go to church or go to an event with a lot of people. The problem is that bad guys tend to ignore laws. Good guys tend to follow laws. Unconstitutional laws such as Michigan's Gun Free Zones only convert the good guys *and* gals into defenseless targets. This is why every state in our nation should be a constitutional carry state.

The next popular target in our Constitution is the Fourth Amendment:

The right of the people to be secure in their persons, houses, papers, and effects, against unreasonable searches and seizures, shall not be violated, and no Warrants shall issue, but upon probable cause, supported by Oath or affirmation, and particularly describing the place to be searched, and the persons or things to be seized.

One of the creepiest examples of how this protection is infringed upon in today's technology-driven society is right out of the pages of George Orwell's classic book *1984*. Picking up where their infringement of our Second Amendment rights left off, cities like New York City have deployed what is referred to as ShotSpotter technology. ShotSpotter is a company that provides gun sensing technology that triangulates the source of a gunshot. It has been used extensively on the battlefield by our military to locate sniper positions. Now, many people want to deploy this technology for civilian use. The sensors used in this technology are simply sophisticated microphones. Microphones tend to pick up more than gunshots when they are turned on. Imagine yourself walking around the block within range of microphones recording your every word. It was creepy enough for my wife and I to discover a phone tap. Try walking into the world of Orwell's Big Brother. Would you feel secure in your person? Even if you have nothing to hide, it wouldn't stop someone from capturing a harmless remark out of context. Trust me. As an elected official, I know of what I speak, whether or not I am within earshot of a microphone on every street corner.

Perhaps the most violated amendments in the Bill of Rights are the Ninth Amendment, which basically says that nothing written in the Constitution can be used to cancel amendments to it, and the Tenth Amendment, which basically says that any power not delegated to the Federal Government and not banned by the Constitution is a power of the states. This gets to the core of the issue brought up at the beginning of this chapter. Our Constitution specifies *limited* powers for the federal government. Yet, our federal government routinely colors outside of the lines of its express authority.

Regrettably, the federal government is not the only unit of government coloring outside of its responsibilities. Prime examples of states and local units of governments ignoring the social compact referred to as our Constitution are the subordination of federal law to Sharia Law and the failure to comply with federal law via what are referred to as Sanctuary State or City policies. Article VI Section 2 of the Constitution is known as the Supremacy Clause. It reads, "This Constitution, and the Laws of the United States which shall be made in Pursuance thereof; and all Treaties made, or which shall be made, under the Authority of the United States, shall be the supreme Law of the Land; and the <u>Judges in every State shall be bound thereby, any Thing in the Constitution or Laws of any State to the Contrary notwithstanding</u>." In other words, our courts are subject to US law not Sharia Law and our states are bound to comply with US law.

Just because I didn't delve into a discussion of *all* of our rights and duties under our Constitution does not mean that other provisions are any less important. It simply means that they have not been subject to as many or as severe of attacks as the ones which I have focused upon. Each of us needs to heed the sage words of our first Supreme Court Chief Justice John Jay who said,

"Every member of the State ought diligently to read and study the constitution of his country. . . . By knowing their rights, they will sooner perceive when they are violated and be the better prepared to defend and assert them."

# 7

# LEADING WITHOUT LEGISLATION

While I have indeed passed my share of important legislation during my tenure in the Michigan Senate, I have found that true servant leadership is about much more than passing legislation. One can make a significant positive difference without having one's name on a bill.

For starters, even though I was the one who took the lead on drafting the Right-to-Work legislation and shepherding it through legal review after legal review, I found it was helpful to let another senator have his name on the legislation as the bill sponsor so that we could add a few very influential senators to the Yes column. Ronald Reagan was absolutely right when he said, "It is amazing what you can get accomplished if you do not care who gets the credit."

Sometimes leadership requires opposition to legislation. Such was the case when my colleagues proposed the so-called Healthy Michigan program (Michigan's euphemism for Section 2001 of Obamacare, also known as Medicaid Expansion, which the governor wholeheartedly supported). I advised my colleagues that there were two ways of expanding access to care for the low-income population. One was to take money from one group of people to subsidize the cost of care for others. The other approach was to lower the cost of delivering quality care. I proposed a solution that pursued the latter course, which I referred to as my Patient-Centered Care Solution. Unfortunately, a majority of my colleagues went on to pursue the former course, despite the fact that Medicaid provided sub-standard coverage at best and the policy of expanding it was fiscally unsustainable. After the federal subsidies for the program would drop off, Michigan taxpayers would be on the hook for over $300 million a year in new taxes to make up the difference. I persistently lobbied my colleagues in the Senate and House. My testimony was so compelling that at one point I was actually barred by the House Speaker and Majority Floor Leader (they supported Medicaid Expansion) from going into the House Chamber to talk with representatives. This action is virtually unprecedented as I was not creating a disturbance on the House Floor. I was merely advising my fellow legislators that there was a better way to achieve the objectives of the legislation that did not involve supporting Obamacare. The legislation was eventually passed in both chambers but not without additional drama on the Senate floor. One needs twenty votes to pass legislation in the Michigan Senate. Proponents of Healthy Michigan had only nineteen votes, seven of which were Republican but one of them was the Senate majority leader. In the case of a 19-19 tie, the lieutenant governor, Brian Calley, would cast the tie-breaking vote. The lieutenant governor had already expressed support for Governor Snyder's signature legislation. As someone who vehemently opposed Obamacare during my campaign for office, I did not want the bill to pass. So I proceeded to keep my vote off of the board yielding a 19-18 vote. This effectively denied the lieutenant governor an opportunity to cast a tie-breaking vote. This parliamentary maneuver worked—at least for three hours. Eventually, they managed to come up with another vote by twisting the arm of one of my Senate colleagues. Sometimes leadership means taking a stand for what is right even if such actions have consequences. In the final analysis, my opposition to this legislation helped drive some conservative provisions into the legislation. In fact, one of these provisions is slated to automatically repeal the legislation in 2020 due to the legislation's failure to save taxpayers money as the proponents of the legislation claimed.

The next policy showdown came in the form of road funding. The initial road funding solution that was passed during the 2014 Lame Duck Session was a $2 billion tax increase proposal known as Proposal 1, which would have increased our sales tax from 6 percent to 7 percent and increased our gas taxes. I was quite vocal in my opposition to this proposal for a variety of reasons. For starters, only about $400 million of the $2 billion tax increase would go to roads—at least at the outset. Furthermore, I had demonstrated numerous alternatives to tax increases for fixing our roads. I provided voters with the information they needed to evaluate the proposal in the form of editorials, town halls, and web postings. I made the case that the key to a sustainable plan for fixing our roads was to build higher quality roads. I went beyond simply saying no and provided a better solution. Proposal 1 was summarily rejected by 81 percent of voters despite its detractors being outspent forty to one. In the wake of the failure of Proposal 1, the Senate majority leader proposed another tax-increase-based proposal within two months of our citizens casting their votes against a tax increase. I opposed this proposal too and took the extraordinary step of challenging any colleague to a debate if they were convinced that tax increases were needed to fix the roads. During deliberations on the House floor for one of the derivatives of the tax-increase-based proposals, I was asked once again to leave the House floor. Different Speaker. Different House majority leader. Same tactic. The tax-based solution to fixing our roads passed over my objection. Less than two years later, there are renewed calls for an additional $2 billion in road funding yet little effort has been expended towards building economical, higher quality roads.

Vocal opposition doesn't always lead to frustration, however. When the governor and some of my colleagues in the Michigan Senate first proposed that we adopt a state-based exchange in support of Obamacare, I once again expressed my opposition. I proceeded to break down the features of a state-based exchange and the similar partnership exchange. I highlighted how both of these options did not result in any significant state control. It was simply an attempt by the federal government to get the states to "paint their fence" to use a Mark Twain analogy. This time these efforts were successful as the House opposed the Senate legislation. In the final analysis, we saved the citizens of Michigan from a policy that cost other states massive amounts of money. In fact, many of them reverted to the federal exchange after wasting hundreds of millions of dollars and countless hours of anxiety for their citizens depending upon a stable health care plan.

Leadership doesn't have to have anything to do with legislation at all. In fact, one of my first acts as a state senator was to team with a dedicated group of selfless veterans to launch what we now call the Freedom Center. As a frequent flier for my consulting business, I have witnessed exceptional support for members of our Armed Forces and veterans in airports throughout the nation.

At our main hub in Michigan, however, the only sign of support was a banner sponsored by local veterans organizations on the way to baggage claim which read Thank You for Your Service. First of all, I thought it would be nice if the sponsor of the sign would have been a group of citizens who were not fellow veterans. After all, veterans are the ones putting their lives on the line so that the rest of us can read the paper at Starbucks, watch our favorite sports team, or sleep soundly at night without the fear of artillery fire. Second of all, I thought it would be nice if we could have a hospitality center like a USO at Detroit Metro Airport.

My Senate team did some digging and found out there was a group of veterans who hosted a hospitality center at the airport during Thanksgiving and Christmas. Before I knew it, I was in communications with Lt. Col. Ken Pratt, USAF (Ret.). Ken was part of a larger group of volunteers that included John McCandless, CAPT USN (Ret.), Howard Rundell, CAPT USN (Ret.), Steve Ihrig, and Gary Herman. Together, we began exploring ways to make the hospitality center a permanent fixture of the airport. After many meetings and hours of planning, we opened our doors on November 11, 2011 at 11:11 a.m. in honor of Veteran's Day. Since our grand opening, hundreds of volunteers and partners have since donated significant time and money to help us fulfill our motto: Serving those who serve us. We now have Freedom Center locations in both terminals at the Detroit Metro Airport and at the Troy and Lansing Military Entrance Processing Stations (MEPS). Since our doors have opened we have helped brighten the day of well over 100,000 active duty personnel, veterans, and their families. It didn't take legislation. It simply took a desire to serve.

Another opportunity to lead presented itself when I heard that the Willow Run Bomber Plant in Ypsilanti was threatened with demolition in 2012. This plant is an icon of the ingenuity of Detroit Automotive Manufacturers and part of the proud history of Michigan as the Arsenal of Democracy during WWII. Henry Ford's team shocked the aviation industry when they demonstrated how to produce one B-24 Liberator Bomber every 55 minutes. The plant is also the home to another icon. The original Rosie the Riveter, Rose "Wil" Monroe, worked at the Willow Run Bomber Plant. The building was under the threat of demolition despite a $6 million campaign to purchase a segment of the old factory. A couple of months before the deadline, Dennis Norton of the Michigan Aerospace Foundation told me they were short about $1.5 million. Due to the historical significance of the plant to most Michiganders, plus its use as a marketing tool to promote our growing Aerospace and Defense industry in the state, I petitioned for the state to fill the gap. My name didn't show up on any bill, but the plant was saved from demolition. Dennis Norton and his fellow caretakers are now refurbishing the building. They are joined in this endeavor by the selfless contributions of numerous foundations plus the labor of Plumbers Union Local 98, International Brotherhood of Electrical Workers 252 and 58, International Union of Painters and Allied Trades, landscaping companies, contractors, and engineers. The project to restore the old Bomber Plant is now reminiscent of an Amish barn-raising that involves everyone in the community. Even General Motors has contributed significant resources to the refurbishment of an old Ford plant. It is so encouraging to see everyone coming together to make this project a success, much as we did back in WWII to win the war. The National Museum of Aviation and

Technology is now able to build the exhibits that will serve as a world class testament to the proud aviation history of this special icon of the Arsenal of Democracy. If you are reading this book and know of someone with a B-24 in need of a loving home, please be sure to reach out to Dennis Norton at the Michigan Aerospace Foundation. It would fit in nicely next to the museum's flightworthy B-17, B-25, and C-47.

In fall 2015, the Michigan State Board of Education set about distributing a proposal for new science and social studies standards for our K-12 classrooms. As someone who serves on the Senate Education Policy Committee, I felt it was important that I understood what standards would be promoted in our schools for the next decade. What I discovered disturbed me greatly.

What concerned me about the proposed standards?[1] For starters, our Science Standards did not encourage instruction in the scientific method. As an engineer from a state renowned for its engineering talent, this was quite disturbing. Our social studies standards were no better. They promoted progressive policies to the exclusion of conservative policies. They promoted LGBTQ issues as civil rights while ignoring the religious conscience rights actually enumerated in our state and US constitutions. They promoted Islam to the exclusion of Christianity, which formed the values upon which our nation was founded. It was quite disturbing to see such a blatant attempt to fundamentally transform America by denying future leaders the complete truth about what makes our nation truly exceptional.

I proceeded to draft two letters to the governor outlining significant issues that I found with the proposed standards. One of the letters identified seven issues with the proposed science standards and suggested remedies. The other letter identified fifteen issues with the proposed social studies standards and suggested remedies. These letters were supported with the signatures of many of my fellow legislators. Upon submittal of the letters, I testified before the State Board of Education to share our collective concerns. The State Board of Education went on to approve the science standards over our objection, but thankfully they did not approve the social studies standards. The Michigan Department of Education proceeded to form a social studies focus group to re-evaluate the standards. I was asked to participate in this group, which took over a year's worth of intense study and discussion. All that I asked of my fellow focus group members was that the standards we adopt were politically neutral and accurate. These objectives were adopted by the focus group. We had some great discussions between people from opposite ends of the political spectrum and worldviews on very sensitive topics. At the end of our deliberations, I am pleased to report that we did indeed reach agreement on resolutions for all fifteen issues I had raised. However, we failed to reach agreement on one issue that surfaced during the discussions. What was that issue? The definition of our core values as Americans. It is no wonder why we do not seem so united as Americans nowadays. We took our collective eyes off the ball regarding civics education and are now paying the price. America is not a land united by our geographic boundaries, any single ethnic background, any single race, or any single creed. America is united by a set of core ideas or values. Once we stop advocating on behalf of the values expressed in our Declaration of Independence and Constitution, we will stop being united.

My service on the Criminal Justice Policy Commission provided me another opportunity to lead without legislation. I was appointed to the board as the Republican Senate representative on the commission. The commission is responsible for collecting, analyzing, and disseminating information regarding state and local sentencing and proposing release policies and incarceration facility capacities. I helped to convert these responsibilities into a tangible action plan.

In addition to having quite a bit of practical experience designing IT solutions, I have a passion for putting "correction" back into the Department of Corrections. It saddens me that some people think of prison as a warehouse as opposed to a place where prisoners can be rehabilitated and become conscientious citizens. There needs to be penalties for violating the law, but we need to do more than lock them up. If we don't, they simply learn how to become better criminals. We need to focus on rehabilitation or else prison simply becomes a revolving door with more victims in its wake. The data collected as a result of the commission's work will help legislators identifying which rehabilitation programs work and which don't.

So far, I've only talked about big policy issues that had statewide implications. Ultimately, though, politics is a about people. It is a about personal interactions with those you serve. These are the moments that I have come to enjoy the most. For example, I love it when students, parents, and teachers come to visit the capitol or when I am invited to visit with them in schools. I try to go beyond the usual "day in the life of a senator" talk and impress upon them the need to understand how our system of government works. I invariably ask students questions like "what is the most accurate term to describe our system of government"? If they say "democracy" or hesitate, I advise them that the word is in our Pledge of Allegiance (i.e., "to the republic"). I go on to ask them to name the five freedoms they are guaranteed under the First Amendment. If they hesitate, I advise them that they are in danger of losing them if they do not know what they are. This tends to get them to think harder.

In the interest of promoting what is noble in our community, I make it a priority to attend Eagle Scout Courts of Honor, celebrations recognizing Scouts who have attained Scouting's highest rank. I often ask the attendees "Wouldn't it be nice if the halls of Lansing or DC adhered to the Scout Oath?" What a different world this would be if we all honored the following pledge, "On my honor, I will do my best to do my duty to God and my country and to obey the Scout Law; to help other people at all times; to keep myself physically strong, mentally awake, and morally straight." When is the last time you were able to describe an elected official as trustworthy, loyal, helpful, friendly, courteous, kind, obedient, cheerful, thrifty, brave, clean, and reverent?

Sometimes public service involves serving as the advocate for a community leader seeking to start a school for underserved students or a pastor converting a building that has sat dormant for a decade into a vibrant church. Sometimes it involves serving as the advocate for a county jailer willing to start a program for wayward teens in need of a safe environment in which to turn around their lives before they get into serious trouble. Sometimes it involves letting local officials know that there are state officials paying attention to how they treat the people they are supposed to serve. Sometimes it simply involves listening to someone going through difficult times and wanting to know they are not alone.

Sometimes public service extends well beyond the boundaries of your district. By networking at events such as WallBuilder's annual Pro-Family Legislators Conference, we have been able to learn from other legislators across the nation and give them encouragement. Through our connections, we have been able to support labor, health care, and education reforms in Missouri, West Virginia, Florida, Nebraska, Pennsylvania, Minnesota, Oklahoma, and Utah. In my quest to find the best policy solutions for our state, I have reached out to other organizations across the country like Docs4Patient Care, American Association of Physicians and Surgeons, American Academy of Family Physicians, and the State Policy Network. I have even contributed to the health care policy debate with popular editorials published at Forbes.com.

A lot of people go into politics because they want to make a difference. Serving as an elected official certainly opens the door to be a difference maker. You don't need to be an elected official, though, to be a leader in your community. If you do choose to run for office, however, it does help to know how our system of government truly works. The next chapter is my attempt to share with you what I have learned about how government really works.

PART 2

# INTRODUCTION TO
# THE SWAMP

# 8

# HOW GOVERNMENT
# REALLY WORKS

When I told people that I was in the middle of writing a book that would explain how government really works, I invariably was asked for a copy when it was completed. I have found there to be an insatiable curiosity about how policies and laws are developed. I have found people are particularly curious about how a politician can promise one thing on the campaign trail but do something completely different once in office.

Perhaps it is the engineer in me, but I am passionate about figuring out how things work. A lot of people claim that the creation of our policies and laws is a lot like the process for making sausage. If you knew how it was made, the end product might not taste as good. For me it is not good enough to look at the end product. I want to know how the sausage is made.

This chapter provides you, the voters, what I have learned about how the sausage is made. So if you are content with enjoying the products of today's political system, I suggest that you skip ahead to the next chapter. If, however, you want to better understand how the process works so that you might better understand how to exert some measure of influence upon it, this chapter is for you.

## THE DESIGN OF THE SYSTEM

In the United States, we live under a republican form of government. In fact, Article IV Section 4 of the United States Constitution guarantees that all of our states have a "republican form of government." This is not a statement about political parties but rather an assertion that citizens of each state are guaranteed to have representation. The word "republic" is derived from the Latin *Rez Publica,* which literally means "representative of the public." Because our representatives are constrained in their actions by the Constitution, the most accurate description of our form of government is that of a constitutional republic. In this section, we will be walking through how state governments are intended to operation within our constitutional republic.

My wife and I are big fans of the CNBC Show *The Profit* featuring Marcus Lemonis. In each episode Mr. Lemonis examines how to improve the operations of a given business as viewed through the lenses of People, Process, and Product. It is the same basic prism through which I examined the business operations of my clients during my eleven-year career as a management consultant. In fact, you will find vestiges of this framework in my first book, *Information Technology Roadmap for Professional Service Firms*.

The People, Process, and Product framework allows us to take a more systematic look at how our constitutional republic is intended to work. By breaking our government into smaller parts, we can better examine how each part works. If we understand how each part works, we will be better able to fix the overall system when it is broken. And I think most of us realize that our system is broken and badly in need of repair.

Rather than delve into a detailed discussion of the roles of the three branches of government, I would rather view government operations as a set of processes to be followed such as how a law is passed or how one gets elected to office. Most students are (or should be) instructed in how our legislative, executive, and judicial branches are supposed to work. What I would like to do is get to the heart of what really happens in the halls of the capitol.

## PEOPLE

Government runs on people power. Just like in sports, each person living under the umbrella of government has a role. Much like my fellow University of Michigan alum Charles Woodson, who found himself playing cornerback one moment, returning punts the next, and running a route as a slot receiver on another play, there are exceptions. The norm, however, is that each person in government is responsible for fulfilling the responsibilities of one of the following positions.

### *Elected Officials*

What exactly is the role of our elected officials? Much of this depends on their specific position in the government. Legislators make laws and pass budgets. Executive branch members are supposed to execute laws. Judicial branch members are supposed to evaluate compliance with a given law. Our system of government breaks down when elected officials stop playing their position or play a position to which they are not assigned.

In order to get a better understanding about what I mean by "playing positions," all you have to do is watch a pee wee hockey or soccer game. Everyone follows the ball.

It is not uncommon to see goalies on the other end of the rink or field trying to score rather than guarding their own net.

Elected officials operate a lot like a pee wee hockey team at times. Many forget about the responsibilities of their position and are simply seeking to score—score a nice pension, score some headlines, or score some votes.

My role as a state senator is captured in my oath of office as provided in our Michigan Constitution: "I do solemnly swear that I will support the Constitution of the United States and the constitution of this state, and that I will faithfully discharge the duties of the office of State Senator according to the best of my ability. So help me God."

Unfortunately, the Michigan Constitution is a little loose on specifics regarding the roles of senators and representatives. In a nutshell, it simply says don't trip over the other branches of government. The US Constitution provides much more clarity on the roles and limits of the legislative branch in Article I, which vests power in Congress.

What all too many government officials lose sight of is their primary role. According to the Declaration of Independence, the primary purpose of government is to secure the rights of the governed. That is why government officials are referred to as public servants. Government is at its worst when our public servants stop acting in the best interests of the public that they were elected to serve.

### Political Parties
Senate and House membership is subdivided into party-specific caucuses. Each caucus elects its own leadership team and

adopts their own caucus-specific rules, which are subordinate to the rules adopted by the respective chambers.

### Leadership

Leadership as it pertains to legislative processes refers principally to the governor, Senate majority leader and Speaker of the House.

Citizens vote for the governor as well as the senators and representatives that make up the legislative branch. What they don't vote for are the Senate majority leader and Speaker of the House. Collectively, I refer to these positions as the Oligarchy. "What the heck is the Oligarchy?" you may be asking. You probably don't recall seeing any check box for an oligarch on your ballot. That's because the average citizen does not vote for an oligarch, at least not directly. Those positions are elected by the majority of senators and representatives respectively.

The Oligarchy controls what bills come up for a vote or what line items will be included in the budget, sets policy direction, serves as primary communications channel to media, determines chairmanships, and influences donations to other elected officials. In short, they are very powerful positions about which most citizens know very little. It would be nice if the selection of these positions were merit based, but, as you will see later in this book, merit is not always the predominant influencing factor for those voting on who holds those leadership positions.

In addition to the Senate majority leader and Speaker, Senate and House members also elect subordinate members of their respective chamber leadership teams. While there may be

variations in terms and authority from state to state, I explain
the different leadership positions found in Michigan's legislative
branch in the four tables below.

## TABLE 1: SENATE MAJORITY LEADERSHIP POSITIONS

| POSITION | RESPONSIBILITIES |
| --- | --- |
| Senate Majority Leader* | The most powerful position in the Senate. Leads the Senate. Leads the Senate majority caucus. Negotiates legislative policies between Senate minority leader, Speaker and governor. Determines committee assignments including chairmanships. Assigns bills to a specific committee. Determines which bills will be placed on agenda and which will not. Manages Senate Majority Communications Office, Senate Majority Policy Office, and nominates non-partisan secretary of the senate. Exerts significant influence over the allocation of Senate majority caucus campaign funds. |
| Senate Majority Floor Leader* | Manages Senate floor operations including the Senate legislative agenda. Second most powerful position in the Senate |
| Assistant Senate Majority Floor Leader | Same as Senate majority floor leader except only presides over floor operations in the absence of the Senate majority floor leader. |
| Senate Appropriations Chair* | Leads Senate deliberations regarding budget matters. Negotiates with Senate appropriations minority vice chair regarding budget priorities. |
| Senator Pro-Tempore* | In many states, the lieutenant governor will preside over the Senate in lieu of the senator pro-tempore. |

| POSITION | RESPONSIBILITIES |
|---|---|
| Assistant Senator Pro-Tempore | Same as senator pro-tempore except only executes such duties in the absence of the senator pro-tempore. |
| Senate Majority Whip | Responsible for confidential determination of Senate majority caucus whip counts on pending legislation. |
| Assistant Senate Majority Whip | Assists Senate majority leader in the determination of Senate majority caucus whip counts. |
| Senate Majority Caucus Chair | Presides over caucus meetings, prepares caucus agenda. |
| Assistant Senate Majority Caucus Chair | Same as majority caucus chair except only presides over caucus meetings in absence of majority caucus chair. |

* This position receives enhanced compensation.

# TABLE 2: SENATE MINORITY LEADERSHIP POSITIONS

| POSITION | DUTIES |
| --- | --- |
| Senate Minority Leader* | The most powerful member of the Senate Minority Caucus. Leader of Senate minority caucus. Principle negotiator with Senate majority leader regarding legislative agenda. Exerts significant influence over the allocation of Senate minority caucus campaign funds. |
| Senate Minority Floor Leader* | Manages minority motions regarding Senate floor operations. |
| Assistant Senate Minority Floor Leader | Same as minority floor leader except only presides over caucus meetings in absence of minority floor leader. |
| Senate Appropriations Minority Vice Chair* | Negotiates Senate minority caucus budget priorities with Senate appropriations chair. |
| Senate Minority Whip | Responsible for confidential determination of Senate minority caucus whip counts on pending legislation. |
| Assistant Senate Minority Whip | Same as Minority floor whip except only whips caucus in absence of minority whip. |
| Senate Minority Caucus Chair | Presides over caucus meetings, prepares caucus agenda. |
| Assistant Senate Minority Caucus Chair | Same as Minority caucus chair except only presides over caucus meetings in absence of minority caucus chair. |

* This position receives enhanced compensation.

# TABLE 3: HOUSE MAJORITY LEADERSHIP POSITIONS

| POSITION | DUTIES |
| --- | --- |
| Speaker of the House* | The most powerful position in the House. Leads the House. Leads the House majority caucus. Negotiates legislative policies between House minority leader, Senate majority leader and governor. Determines committee assignments including chairmanships, assigns bills to a specific committee. Determines which bills will be placed on agenda and which will not. Manages House majority communications office, House majority policy office. Nominates non-partisan secretary of the House. Exerts significant influence over the allocation of House majority caucus campaign funds. |
| House Majority Floor Leader* (Typically used as stepping stone for Senate majority leader.) | Manages House floor operations including House legislative agenda. |
| Assistant House Majority Floor Leader | Same as House majority floor leader except only presides over floor operations in the absence of the House majority floor leader. |
| House Appropriations Chair* | Leads House deliberations regarding budget matters. Negotiates with House appropriations minority vice chair regarding budget priorities. |
| House Majority Whip | Responsible for confidential determination of House majority caucus whip counts on pending legislation. |

| POSITION | DUTIES |
| --- | --- |
| Assistant House Majority Whip | Assists House majority leader in the determination of House majority caucus whip counts. |
| House Majority Caucus Chair | Presides over caucus meetings, prepares caucus agenda. |
| Assistant House Majority Caucus Chair | Same as majority caucus chair except only presides over caucus meetings in absence of majority caucus chair |

* This position receives enhanced compensation.

## TABLE 4: HOUSE MINORITY LEADERSHIP POSITIONS

| POSITION | DUTIES |
| --- | --- |
| House Minority Leader* | The most powerful member of the House minority caucus.<br>Leader of Senate minority caucus.<br>Principle negotiator with House majority leader regarding legislative agenda.<br>Exerts significant influence over the allocation of House minority caucus campaign funds. |
| House Minority Floor Leader* | Manages minority motions regarding House floor operations. |
| Assistant House Minority Floor Leader | Same as Minority floor leader except only presides over caucus meetings in absence of Minority floor leader |
| House Appropriations Chair* | Negotiates Senate minority caucus budget priorities with House appropriations chair. |
| House Minority Whip | Responsible for confidential determination of House minority caucus whip counts on pending legislation. |
| Assistant House Minority Whip | Same as Minority floor whip except only presides over caucus meetings in absence of minority whip. |

| POSITION | DUTIES |
|---|---|
| House Minority Caucus Chair | Presides over caucus meetings, prepares caucus agenda. |
| Assistant House Minority Caucus Chair | Same as minority caucus chair except only presides over caucus meetings in absence of minority caucus chair. |

* This position receives enhanced compensation.

The leadership teams are intended to represent the inner circle of decision makers for the Senate majority leader, Senate minority leader, speaker of the House, or House minority leader. They are in essence trusted advisors. In this capacity, they are supposed to represent the interests of the remaining caucus members who elected them to these positions by advising the respective leaders of each caucus how to proceed on policy and other political matters. How these leadership teams operate in practice, however, varies significantly as a function of the leadership style of the respective caucus leader.

During my tenure as the assistant majority caucus chair, we would meet weekly to review policy strategy. Sometimes the leader would look for advice on how to proceed but more often than not, he would use the meeting to practice his messaging to the caucus on decisions that had already been made.

### Committees

Committees are designed to be where the merits of a given piece of legislation are evaluated. This doesn't always happen. Committee chairs preside over the deliberations of their assigned committee. The degree of deliberation on a given bill is controlled by the committee chair. Bills can sail through committee without any discussion or be the subject of prolonged discussion. It is during committees that most amendments or bill substitutes are introduced to improve legislation based on the assessments of committee members. Committees can also be held independent of the consideration of any piece of legislation. When I served as chair of the State Police and Military Affairs Appropriations Subcommittees we used to conduct quarterly reviews of performance metrics to see if any midcourse budget corrections were warranted.

Committee chairs can be powerful roles, depending on the committee and the legislation routed to the committee by the Senate Majority Leader. Committee chairs can effectively kill a bill by refusing to hear testimony on it. Bills cannot receive a vote on the floor unless they have been reported favorably from a committee or enough members vote on the chamber floor to discharge the bill from the committee to the chamber floor. Most discharge motions require the approval of the Senate Majority Leader who more often than not put the bill into a specific committee with full knowledge of whether or not there was sufficient support for the bill in that committee.

The list of committees within a given legislative chamber can vary significantly from state to state or even from legislative session to legislative session. The current Michigan Senate committees are listed on the following page.

# SENATE COMMITTEES

Agriculture
Appropriations

## APPROPRIATIONS SUBCOMMITTEES

| | |
|---|---|
| Agriculture and Rural Development | Capital Outlay |
| Community Colleges | Corrections |
| Environmental Quality | General Government |
| Health and Human Services | Higher Education |
| Judiciary | K-12, School Aid, Education |
| Licensing and Regulatory Affairs | Natural Resources |
| State Police and Military Affairs | Transportation |

Banking and Financial Institutions
Commerce
Economic Development and International Investment
Education
Elections and Government Reform
Energy and Technology
Families, Seniors, and Human Services
Finance
Government Operations
Health Policy
Insurance
Judiciary
Local Government
Michigan Competiveness
Natural Resources
Outdoor Recreation and Tourism
Oversight
Regulatory Reform
Transportation

Veterans, Military Affairs, and Homeland Security

### Lobbyists

Lobbyists are called that because they often can be seen in the lobbies of each chamber within the capitol during important votes. Many lobbyists are former elected officials. There are many different types of lobbyists, but they basically fall into the following two classes: Multi-client and special interest. Lobbyists can play an extremely valuable role as subject matter experts. They often hold significant institutional knowledge that can lend insight as to why a certain policy is written the way it is. They know how the system works.

Lobbyists often get a bad reputation because they often practice pay-to-play politics, or providing financial incentive for political gain. These tactics only work if the elected officials play this game. It is the responsibility of the elected officials to say no and focus on the best interest of their constituents. In other words, lobbyists are not the problem in politics. Elected officials who listen to lobbyists more than they listen to their constituents are the problem. Elected officials are supposed to serve as the lobbyists for the best interests of the citizens. Sadly, this is often the exception and not the rule.

### Media

There are many different types of media: TV, radio, print, online, and even social media. The media has a constitutionally protected role in America because an informed citizenry is critical to the success of our constitutional republic. In order for our republic to work effectively, the media needs to provide an unbiased, accurate account of the service of our representatives to the people whom they represent.

Unfortunately, many in the media seek to abuse this authority and taint their coverage of the news and even the selection of what news is covered to fit their own worldview. Such behavior by the media is exactly why President Trump and others announce that many news outlets are providing fake news rather than unbiased, accurate reporting. Media buys are typically the most expensive line item in any campaign budget, so when one party or one worldview dominates the existing media channels, it amounts to virtually unlimited free advertising for that party or worldview.

I have coined the phrase Mad Lib Journalism for any news story in which reporters already have written the story and is simply looking for a few colorful adjectives to give the appearance that they considered all sides to the story.

The sad fact of the matter is that today, when our citizens have access to more information than ever before, it is more important than ever to do your own investigation. Today more than ever, there is no substitute for a vigilant citizenry willing to roll up their sleeves and seek the truth by going directly to the source.

### Donors

Donors are very influential players in government. Donors act as gatekeepers. Donors dictate key committee assignments. Donors dictate key policy working group members. Donors dictate which policies will be brought up for a vote.

Major donors are typically lobbyists, but there are also key party loyalists who do not serve officially as lobbyists. If your policy perspective is not in sync with those of influential donors, you will be excluded from the process no matter how hard you attempt to assert your perspective.

*Citizens*

Citizens are the customers for the fruits of government. In our republican form of government, our primary role as citizens is to elect those who represent us in office. Occasionally, we participate directly in the approval of the products of government via ballot initiatives, but this is the exception not the rule.

## PROCESS

In my career I would often describe my designs in operations manuals by way of a process diagrams. The manuals captured the *intended* use of my designs, not all possible uses. In much the same way, I have attempted to capture the basic operations of government in process diagrams. Mind you, these are also the *intended* operations, not all possible operations. Later in this book, I will attempt to differentiate between some of these intended operations and other operations which I have observed. For the time being, let's take a look at how some of our key government processes are supposed to work.

*Elections*

I could easily dedicate an entire book to how elections work— or at least are supposed to work. Most elections feature both a primary election and a general election. In primary elections, the candidate who will represent the party in the general election is typically chosen by voters who are members of that respective party. Once the respective party candidates have been chosen during the primary election, registered voters then vote in a general election featuring no more than one candidate per party as well as independent candidates. There are two basic types of primary elections: open and closed. During an open primary, registered voters can cast their vote on either party's ballot. In a closed primary, voters must register with a given party before being allowed to vote in the pertinent party's primary election.

Before a candidate ever gets on a ballot, however, he or she has a lot of work to do. The first formal step in the process is to file for office by submitting a campaign filing with the pertinent clerk's office. Each state's requirement is different, so you will have to refer to your state's election bureau for details on how to file for office in your state. Depending on the position, you may need to submit a filing fee, petition signatures, or both, in order to get on the ballot. This is only the beginning of the process. In order to collect signatures or the filing fee, one often needs money. In fact, some candidates for statewide offices in Michigan have been known to pay as much as $6 per signature to help them get on the ballot in a timely manner. If you are not independently wealthy or supported by a large number of volunteers, you will need to collect money to do so.

In order to collect money, one needs a bank account. Essentially, one needs to run a campaign as a business. This business, however, has its own complicated set of rules and regulations governed by campaign finance laws. While all of this infrastructure is being setup, the candidate also needs to be out in public boosting name recognition and kissing babies.

As Figure 2 on page 105 indicates, elections involve much more than voting and candidates kissing babies. Behind the scenes, there are many important stakeholders of whom most voters may not even be aware.

One of my biggest surprises when I first ran for office was the virtual deluge of questionnaires that I received from various special-interest organizations. These questionnaires could be as simple as a one-page true-false exam or a complex multi-page, essay contest. The responses to these questionnaires may or may not lead to endorsements and financial contributions. Responses are often very time consuming, so candidates must be discerning as to which questionnaires they respond to and how. After all, time is one of the most precious commodities any candidate has on the campaign trail.

Ultimately, elections are not about how much money a candidate raises. They are not about how many doors you've knocked. They are not about how many times you appear on TV. They are about votes. The candidate with the most votes wins.

### *Leadership Elections*

Earlier, I discussed the important roles of the governor, Senate majority leader and Speaker of the House. Everyone knows how the governor is determined: a direct vote of the people. Many of you are probably wondering, however, who elects the Senate majority leader and Speaker of the House. The Senate majority leader is elected by the newly elected state senators who will be serving in the subsequent legislative session. The Speaker of the House is elected by the newly elected state representatives who will be serving in the subsequent legislative session. Technically, they are elected by all of the legislators in each elected body. In practice, however, they are elected by the party with a majority of members in either chamber as the nominations are typically unanimous within party ranks.

Contrary to the very public nature of the elections of the governor, state senators, and state representatives, you won't see any yard signs or receive any robo calls regarding the races for

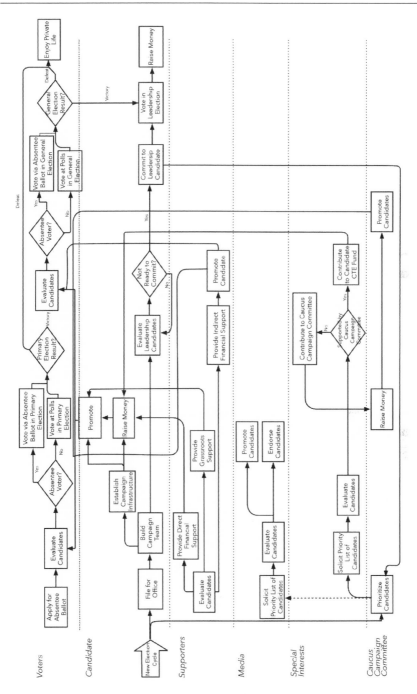

**Figure 2 Election Process**

Senate majority leader or Speaker of the House. These elections are very much clandestine affairs involving big donors and internal party politics.

Unlike in the primaries and general elections, polls in leadership elections are almost as good as votes in leadership elections as each leadership candidate seeks a personal commitment from each senator or representative in his or her respective caucus. I say almost because not all senators or representatives can be trusted to follow through on their commitments. These early commitments are typically based on a political calculation performed by each prospective official. The true commitments are revealed shortly after the general election when a meeting is convened between all of the successful candidates of a given party. At this meeting, each member who will serve in the upcoming legislature casts a vote for the various leadership positions. The party with the most caucus members in their respective chamber selects from the majority leadership positions. The party with the fewest caucus members in their respective chamber selects from the minority leadership positions. These positions are then formalized by motions and votes in each respective chamber.

### Passing Legislation

One of the primary functions of the legislative branch is to evaluate and pass legislation. Typically, the successful passage of legislation means that a bill has earned the support of the majority of members in each legislative chamber and the governor. In Michigan, there are 110 representatives, 38 senators, and 1 governor. This translates to a 56-20-1 formula for passing legislation corresponding to fifty-six representatives, twenty senators, and one governor. If a bill does not have the support of

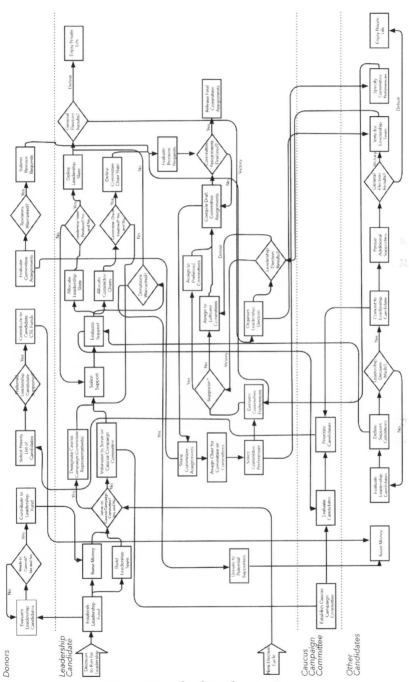

*Figure 3 Leadership Election Process*

the governor, the legislature needs a super majority of two-thirds of each chamber to override the veto of the governor in order for a bill to become a law. In Michigan this translates to 74-26 votes.

Before legislation gets to that point, though, there are quite a few steps that need to be taken, not the least of which is the drafting the legislation. Legislation is typically not drafted by legislators but by experts. In Michigan most bills are drafted by the Legislative Services Bureau. Drafts are reviewed by the bill sponsor and his or her staff until the language is ready to be introduced as a bill.

Once a bill has been introduced, it is read into the public record, assigned a bill number, and typically referred to a committee for consideration. If successfully reported from committee, in the Michigan Senate it goes to what is referred to as the Committee of the Whole for deliberation by the complete chamber. Once approved by the Committee of the Whole, the legislation is considered by the entire chamber body. Throughout the process, legislators can propose amendments or bill substitutes for consideration by the body.

Once approved by the majority of members in the first chamber, the bill goes to the other chamber whereby the process repeats itself. If both chambers pass the bill, it goes to the governor for consideration.

In case you are thinking that this budget process is way too complex, keep in mind this flow chart merely scratches the surface of what it takes to pass a piece of legislation. There are many nuances not factored in here that often need to be taken into consideration especially for contentious pieces of legislation. It is best to refer to a state's constitution to gain a more in-depth understanding of the legislative process. Suffice it to say, though,

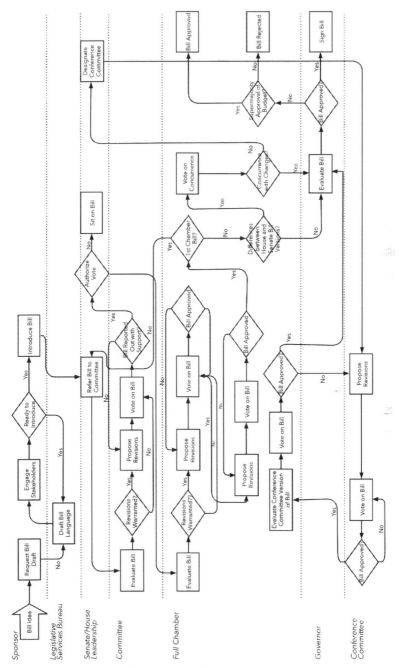

*Figure 4 Legislative Process*

under our system of government, it *should* be difficult to pass legislation. Every piece of legislation typically means yet another constraint on our freedom. Constraints on our freedom should not be added lightly.

### Passing Budgets

Budgets are a special type of legislation often with special constitutional provisions specific to budgets. For example, unlike policy legislation, the governor actually kicks off the budget process in Michigan with a budget proposal. Michigan has another wrinkle in the process: the requirement of balanced budgets. A revenue estimating conference report establishes the starting constraint for the executive budget. The revenue estimate is then updated on a quarterly basis. Each time it is updated, budget proposals that reflect the latest figures are submitted for votes. Budgets represent the single most powerful tool in the ability of the legislature to hold state agencies accountable.

### Floor Sessions

One of the basic responsibilities of legislators is to participate in floor sessions. Floor sessions are when legislators of all parties come together to cast their formal votes on legislation and conduct other business on behalf of the entire chamber. Michigan is one of ten states with full-time legislatures. Because of this, we have floor sessions throughout the year. Other states have part-time legislatures in which sessions are limited to a specific time span during the year or even every other year.

The conduct of the floor sessions is governed by the rules of each respective chamber as adopted independently by each

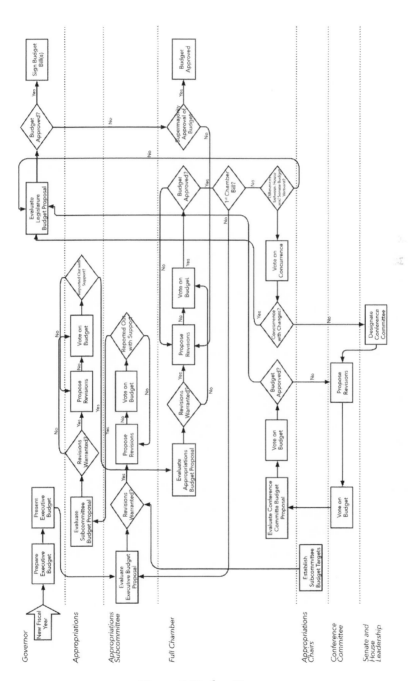

*Figure 5 Budget Process*

chamber. Each chamber follows a standard agenda for each floor session although the order of the agenda can typically be modified to suit the circumstance of the floor action for a given day.

The standard Michigan Senate floor agenda is as follows:

- Invocation
- Pledge of Allegiance
- Introduction and Referral of Bills
- Resolutions
- Messages from the Governor
- Messages from the House
- General Orders
- Third Reading
- Statements
- Adjournment

Among the rules invoked in the Michigan Senate is that of a "shot clock" for roll-call votes. Senators have one minute to register their vote once the "board" is opened by the secretary of the Senate. In the House, there is no shot clock; the board can stay open for days or seconds. Once adjourned, the Senate chamber will cease deliberations until the next session day.

If you would really like to do a deep dive into how Floor Sessions operate, I recommend reading the rules adopted by the respective chamber of interest. It provides a smorgasbord of procedural nuances that often make for an interesting read for serious politicos.

### Committee Hearings

Committees are designed to be the mechanism for substantive deliberation on each piece of legislation assigned to the committee by the Senate majority leader. Once assigned, committee chairs decide which bills will be discussed, when they will be discussed (if at all), who will discuss the bill, and in what order. As you can see, committee chairmanships can be extremely powerful positions.

During committee hearings, the bill sponsor or their delegate will provide a summary of the legislation and make their case for why the bill should be supported. Bill detractors are also given time to state their case why the bill should not be supported. Committee members are encouraged to ask questions of those providing testimonies so as to better discern the impacts of the legislation. Committee members can also amend legislation as necessary to address any concerns they might have. If the amendments are adopted by a majority of the committee members, they are included in the version of the bill that is considered for passage by the committee. If the majority of the committee members find the legislation acceptable, the bill is "reported" to the floor for further consideration by the entire legislative body, or to a parent committee if it is being considered in a subcommittee. If legislation has not earned the support of a majority of committee members, the bill can still be "discharged" from committee by way of a floor session motion subject to the support of the majority of legislators in the respective chamber.

As with floor sessions, each committee adopts its own set of rules for committee hearings.

## PRODUCTS

In most respects, our government operates much like any other professional service firm. Each branch of government provides a specified list of services.

### Legislative Services

The services provided by the legislative branch include the creation or modification of laws and the passing of budgets plus various oversight functions. State legislators are authorized to pass only legislation that is defined by the pertinent state constitution in much the same way that Article I Section 8 of the United States Constitution is supposed to limit the scope of federal legislation.

When most citizens think of legislation, they think of policy bills. Policy bills amend the compiled laws of the state which in turn give guidance to law enforcement officers and judges regarding what constitutes a crime. These are the most prevalent forms of legislation, but they are not the only type of legislation. Table 5 provides a more comprehensive list of legislation types.

As alluded to in the previous chapter, legislators have the opportunity to do much more than pass legislation. Due to their position of influence, they can impact communities in many ways besides the passage of legislation.

### Executive Services

The executive branch is responsible for "executing" the services established in law by the Constitution and legislative action. The job of running the government is a full-time job. These services are executed by way of various agencies established in state governance. Table 6 provides a list of the state agencies found within Michigan's executive branch.

## TABLE 5: TYPES OF LEGISLATION

| LEGISLATION TYPE | DESCRIPTION | EXAMPLE |
| --- | --- | --- |
| Policy Bill | Legislation that modifies the compiled laws for the state. | A bill to make it illegal to assault someone. |
| Appropriations Bill | Legislation that authorizes line item expenditures on behalf of state. | A bill to authorize FY18 expenditures for the attorney general's office. |
| Resolution | A chamber-specific resolution providing special recognition on a topic deemed important by a sponsoring legislator that does not need approval by both chambers. Most resolutions are simply gaveled into the journal without a roll call vote. | A resolution to make paper clips the official state office supply. |
| Joint Resolution | A legislative measure requiring the approval of both chambers* which carries the force of law. Joint resolutions often require a supermajority of legislators in each chamber to pass. | A resolution to propose an amendment to the state or federal Constitution. |
| Concurrent Resolution | A legislative measure that, once approved, expresses the intent of both chambers that is not enforceable. Concurrent resolutions are essentially letters on behalf of the majority of legislators in both chambers. | A resolution requesting that the federal government expand allowable Health Savings Account expenses to include direct primary care services. |

* In all states except Nebraska there is a bicameral legislature consisting of a Senate and House (although the terms for each may vary from state to state). Nebraska has a unicameral legislature.

# TABLE 6: STATE OF MICHIGAN EXECUTIVE BRANCH DEPARTMENTS

| DEPARTMENT | DESCRIPTION |
| --- | --- |
| **Agriculture and Rural Development** | The mission of the Michigan Department of Agriculture & Rural Development is to "assure the food safety, agricultural, environmental, and economic interests of the people of the State of Michigan are met through service, partnership and collaboration." |
| **Attorney General** | The attorney general is the lawyer for the State of Michigan. When public legal matters arise, he renders opinions on matters of law and provides legal counsel for the legislature and for each officer, department, board, and commission of state government. He provides legal representation in court actions and assists in the conduct of official hearings held by state agencies. |
| **Civil Rights** | The Department of Civil Rights, in implementing the mission of the commission, secures the full enjoyment of civil rights guaranteed by law and the constitution through the elimination of discrimination. This is accomplished through the investigation and resolution of complaints of discrimination, outreach and education programs designed to promote voluntary compliance with civil rights laws, mediation, referral, crisis intervention, anti-hate crime programming, and the dissemination of information which explains citizen rights and responsibilities provided in a legal framework. |
| **Civil Service Commission** | The Civil Service Commission has overall responsibility for regulating conditions of employment for classified civil service workers in all of the departments of the executive branch of state government. |

| DEPARTMENT | DESCRIPTION |
|---|---|
| **Corrections** | The Department of Corrections administers Michigan's adult prison, probation, and parole systems. The department has jurisdiction over all adults convicted of felonies who are sentenced to prison. Convicted felons who are not sentenced to prison terms are either sentenced to a county jail term or are supervised in the community through a system called probation. Probation services for felons are provided by the department for the various felony courts in Michigan's counties. |
| **Education** | The Department of Education, under the direction of the superintendent of public instruction, carries out the policies of the State Board of Education. The department implements federal and state legislative mandates in education. |
| **Environmental Quality** | The department is dedicated to protecting human health and to preserving a healthy environment. The department will exemplify good environmental stewardship and affirm that a healthy environment is critical to our social, cultural, and economic well-being. The department will protect human health and the environment while fostering a healthy economy by effective and efficient administration of agency programs, and by providing for use of innovative strategies. This is being accomplished in a manner that is rebuilding the integrity of the department as an environmental protection agency that carries out this mission in a professional, just, and productive manner. |
| **Health and Human Services** | The Michigan Department of Health and Human Services strives to promote better health outcomes, reduce health risks, and support stable and safe families while encouraging self-sufficiency. |

| DEPARTMENT | DESCRIPTION |
| --- | --- |
| **Insurance and Financial Services (DIFS)** | The Department of Insurance and Financial Services (DIFS) is responsible for regulating Michigan's financial industries, including banks, credit unions, insurance, mortgage companies, and other consumer finance lenders. |
| **Licensing and Regulatory Affairs** | The Department of Licensing and Regulatory Affairs (LARA) supports business growth and job creation while safeguarding Michigan's citizens through a simple, fair, efficient and transparent regulatory structure. |
| **Military and Veterans Affairs** | The Department of Military and Veterans Affairs, also known as the state military establishment, has three primary missions: to execute the duties laid down by various statutes and the governor, administration of state-supported veterans programming, and military preparedness to assist both state and federal authorities. The Michigan Army and Air National Guard constitute the armed forces of the state and serve under the orders of the governor as commander-in-chief. The governor appoints an adjutant general to serve as commanding general of the Michigan National Guard and as director of the Department of Military and Veterans Affairs. |
| **Natural Resources (DNR)** | The Michigan Department of Natural Resources is committed to the conservation, protection, management, use and enjoyment of the state's natural and cultural resources for current and future generations. |
| **Secretary of State** | The Department of State is the oldest department of Michigan state government and is administered by the secretary of state. Elected to a four-year term, the secretary of state is a member of the executive branch of government and has constitutional as well as statutory duties. |

| DEPARTMENT | DESCRIPTION |
|---|---|
| **State Police** | The purpose of the department is to provide twenty-four-hour statewide quality police service for the safety and protection of the people and their property in the state of Michigan. Its primary responsibilities are to reduce the opportunities for crime, to reduce traffic accidents through diligent and fair enforcement of the laws of this state, and to act as a first responder to any citizen's needs that can be addressed through the resources of the criminal justice system. |
| **Talent and Economic Development** | Joining job creation and economic development efforts under one umbrella, the Department of Talent and Economic Development consists of the Michigan Economic Development Corporation, the Michigan State Housing Development Authority, the Michigan Strategic Fund and the newly created Talent Investment Agency (TIA). TED allows the state to leverage its ability to build talent with in-demand skills while helping state businesses grow and thrive. |
| **Technology, Management and Budget** | The Department of Technology, Management and Budget promotes a unified approach to information technology management and provides centralized administration of services including auditing, budgeting, employee resources, financial services, fleet management, mail, printing, property management, purchasing, records management, and retirement services for departments and agencies in the executive branch of state government. |

| DEPARTMENT | DESCRIPTION |
|---|---|
| **Transportation** | The primary functions of the Department of Transportation are the construction, improvement, and maintenance of the state highway system—the 9,620 miles of interstate, U.S.- and M-numbered highways—and the administration of other state transportation programs. Responsibilities include the development and implementation of comprehensive transportation plans for the entire state, including aeronautics and bus and rail transit, providing professional and technical assistance, and the administration of state and federal funds allocated for these programs. The director of the department is appointed by the governor, with the advice and consent of the senate. |
| **Treasury** | Treasury exists to provide quality financial, tax, and administrative services. The state treasurer acts as principal advisor to the governor on tax and fiscal policy issues. The state treasurer is the chairperson of the Michigan Debt Advisory Board, the Michigan Education Trust, the Michigan Higher Education Assistance Authority, the Michigan Higher Education Student Loan Authority, the Michigan Merit Award Board, the Michigan Municipal Bond Authority, and the Michigan School District Accountability Board. |

**SOURCE:** Michigan.gov

### *Judicial Services*

The Judicial Branch is responsible for evaluating compliance with the laws in response to lawsuits.

# TYPES OF COURTS IN THE STATE OF MICHIGAN

## APPELLATE
### *Supreme Court*

The Supreme Court is a state's court of last resort. In Michigan, the Supreme Court consists of seven justices. The Supreme Court receives applications for leave to appeal from litigants primarily seeking review of decisions by the Court of Appeals.

The Supreme Court's authority to hear cases is discretionary. The Court grants leave to those cases of greatest complexity and public import, where additional briefing and oral argument are essential to reaching a just outcome.

Each justice is responsible for reviewing each case to determine whether leave should be granted. Cases that are accepted for oral argument may be decided by an order, with or without an opinion. These orders may affirm or reverse decisions by the Court of Appeals, may remand a case to the trial court, or may adopt a correct Court of Appeals opinion.

Cases come before the Court during a limited time frame each year. During this timeframe, the Court hears oral arguments. Decisions are released throughout the term, following oral arguments.

In addition to its judicial duties, the Supreme Court is responsible for the general administrative supervision of all courts in the state. The Supreme Court also establishes rules for practice and procedure in all courts.[*]

---

[*]    SOURCE: Courts.Michigan.gov

## Court of Appeals

The Court of Appeals is what is known as an appellate court. Generally, decisions from final orders of a circuit court, as well as some probate court and agency orders, may be appealed to the court as a matter of right. Other lower court or tribunal decisions may be appealed only by application for leave to appeal, i.e., with permission of the court. The court also has jurisdiction to hear some original actions, such as complaints for mandamus or superintending control against government officers or actions alleging that state law has imposed an unfunded or inadequately funded mandate on local units of government.[**] The Court of Appeals does not typically support trial by jury.

## CIVIL

## Court of Claims

The Court of Claims is a court of statewide, limited jurisdiction to hear and determine all civil actions filed against the state and its agencies. These cases include highway defect, medical malpractice, contracts, constitutional claims, prisoner litigation, tax-related suits, and other claims for monetary damages.[***]

## TRIAL

## Circuit Court

The circuit court is the trial court with the broadest powers. In Michigan, the circuit court typically handles all civil cases with claims of more than $25,000 and all felony criminal cases (cases where the accused, if found guilty, could be sent to prison). The family division of circuit court handles all cases regarding divorce,

---

[**]    SOURCE: Courts.Michigan.gov

[***]   SOURCE: Courts.Michigan.gov

paternity, adoptions, personal protection actions, emancipation of minors, treatment and testing of infectious disease, safe delivery of newborns, name changes, juvenile offenses and delinquency, juvenile guardianship, and child abuse and neglect. In addition, the circuit court hears cases appealed from the other trial courts or from administrative agencies. The friend of the court office is part of the family division of the circuit court and handles domestic relations cases where minor children are involved.****

### District Court

The district court is often called the people's court. More people have contact with the district court than any other court. The district court handles most traffic violations, all civil cases with claims up to $25,000, landlord-tenant matters, most traffic tickets, and all misdemeanor criminal cases (generally, cases where the accused, if found guilty, cannot be sentenced to more than one year in jail). In addition, small claims cases are heard by a division of the district court.

### Municipal Court

In Michigan, a few municipalities have chosen to retain a municipal court rather than create a district court. The municipal courts have limited powers

### Probate Court

The probate court handles wills, administers estates and trusts, appoints guardians and conservators, and orders treatment for mentally ill and developmentally disabled persons.

****  SOURCE: Michigan Courts: http://courts.mi.gov/courts/trialcourts/pages/default.aspx.

### Specialty Courts

Specialty courts are innovative programs designed to address an offender's underlying problem and improve the likelihood of returning the offender as a productive member of society once the sentence has been served. Specialty courts have been formed in Michigan to address the special circumstances associated with drugs, mental health, and veterans.

To this point of the book, we have focused upon how the system is supposed to operate. In the next chapter, we will start to examine how it works in practice.

# 9

# SWAMP PRIORITIES

Jesse Marvin Unruh was a well-known Democratic Politician and the California State Treasurer from 1975 to 1987. He seemed to have a good understanding of politics when he said, "Money is the mother's milk of politics."

Have you ever wondered why bad bills seem to get passed when perfectly good bills disappear into black holes? This part of the book will lend some insights into why this is so.

During my tenure as a state senator in Michigan, Republicans have had a supermajority in the Senate, a majority in the House, and the governorship, yet bills that aligned with the Republican platform went nowhere while bills that were antithetical to that platform progressed. Two notable examples are Medicaid Expansion and what is referred to as the Senior Pension Tax.

Medicaid Expansion implements section 2001 of HR 3590 aka Obamacare. The slogan Repeal Obamacare was forcefully shouted from the hilltops by pretty much every Republican candidate for office in Michigan, as well as nationwide. So what did Michigan do? We implemented Medicaid Expansion and branded it "Healthy Michigan." We even did so in the face of free-market alternatives that would have expanded access to care for low-income individuals without breaking the back of taxpayers.

The Senior Pension Tax is another obvious deviation from the Republican platform plank of lower taxes. Michigan needed to balance its budget. Instead of pursuing ways of reducing expenses either by improving the delivery of existing services or by cutting unnecessary programs, the only solution that was entertained by Republican leadership was a tax increase. They later pursued the same myopic approach to fixing Michigan's roads via a gas tax and registration fee hike.

Republican leadership was completely tone deaf to its base, which by and large voted for Republicans because of the principles embodied in our platform.

Democrats are no better.

While there are indeed very stark differences between the Republican and Democrat platforms, the fact is that there is very little difference between how Republicans and Democrats work the system.

In the 2016 presidential election the interim DNC Chairman, Donna Brazile, colluded with Hillary Clinton during the Democratic primary by giving her debate questions in advance. This is but one example of how the Swamp seeks to protect its own. Another example of this protection mindset is the concept of unelected super delegates. Super delegates are yet another Swamp mechanism to silence the voice of the voters. During presidential primaries, the Democratic Party allows unelected super delegates to vote for whatever candidate they choose, thus evading the will of the people. The vast majority of these super delegates went to Hillary Clinton despite Bernie Sanders receiving significant support from Democratic voters.

Why are both parties so tone deaf?

The simple answer is that government is run by people and people are not perfect—not a single one of them including myself (see Romans 3:23). It is a sad facet of life that government positions appeal to the most base human desires: power and security. We all seek significance, power, and financial security. Those who enter politics with a strong moral compass have to fight the temptation to grab more power and more financial gain. Those without morals who enter into higher politics usually feed those desires at the expense of everyone else's pursuit of significance, power, and financial security. Our Founders recognized this when they designed our system to be a *limited* government. The less power given to those in government, the less opportunity they have to mess with the lives of those whom they were elected to serve.

In retrospect, my first clue as to how government really works was when Angie and I met with Michigan GOP representatives responsible for Senate and House campaigns. We came into the meeting ready to discuss how we firmly believed in the Republican principles of constitutionally limited government, personal responsibility, and the sanctity of life. We were ready to talk about how my experience as an engineer, management consultant, and small business owner would be a great asset as a problem-solver in the Senate. Their first question, though, was not about our values or experience. It was "how much money can you raise for your campaign?"

It should have dawned on us at that moment that everything in politics revolved around money. It didn't. Perhaps we were still a bit too idealistic. After all, everything in politics shouldn't revolve around money. It should be based on principles and

values. We are called the United States of America because we are
supposed to be united behind shared principles and values. We
should be focusing on how to solve the problems that we face in
a manner consistent with these principles and values. That is how
our political system was designed to work. Unfortunately, that is
not how it is working.

In order to differentiate between how our government was
originally intended to work and how it actually works, it is fitting
to use the term "Swamp" in reference to how it actually works.
After all, swamps are dark, dank, and murky environments. It
is often difficult to see the path ahead. Even when you can see
where you are going, you can still get stuck in the mud. To make
matters worse, around every bend, behind every stump, there
are plenty of snakes and alligators ready to defend their turf to
the death. In short, the Swamp is not known for sunshine and
lollipops.

So what exactly are the denizens of the Swamp seeking to
defend? They are seeking to defend a system within our system
that has a radically different set of priorities from those of our
Founders. These priorities ranked in order are to:

1. Special interests who may have contributed
   financially to their campaigns
2. Senate and House leadership
3. Fulfilling campaign promises
4. Party platform
5. Best interests of our citizens at large

Ultimately, these priorities serve to protect the financial
interests of Swamp residents to the detriment of our citizens at
large.

Is it any wonder as to why the messages Drain the Swamp (President Trump), Make DC Listen (Senator Cruz), or Not for Sale (Senator Sanders) resonated with so many of us in the last presidential election? It is because the best interests of citizens are at the bottom of the priority list.

In a nutshell, money is what drives political decisions: decisions about which bills get a vote, about which members get chairmanships of which committee, about what budget line items are adopted and which are not, about which candidates get financial support and which don't, about who is elected to leadership to make those decisions ostensibly on behalf of their caucus members. Money is indeed the energy that keeps the Swamp alive and kicking.

Why does money have so much influence? Money purchases airtime on TV or radio to promote a candidate or policy. Money is also used by prospective Senate majority leaders or Speakers to secure the favor of the majority of their prospective caucus members by providing them with the financial resources needed to purchase airtime for their elections.

One's natural reaction to this observation is to say, "Just take the money out of politics." In an ideal world, that would be an excellent suggestion. We do not live in an ideal world, however. The scope of the Swamp's influence extends well beyond campaign finance statements.

Let's start by looking at how to promote fairness with airtime. Most people recognize that our media has significant bias. CNN has been referred to pejoratively as the Clinton News Network. The bias isn't just conjecture. It was proven when WikiLeaks released Hillary's emails proving that CNN favored her in the

2018 presidential primaries by providing her the debate questions in advance.

The influence of money goes much deeper than media bias, however. Have you ever wondered why virtual monopolies, such as regulated utilities, spend a significant amount of money on TV, radio, and print advertising? They do this so media companies will come to depend on their ad revenue. This dependence ensures the utility company good press; it discourages stories that might reflect negatively on the quality or value of the services they provide. Is there any limit on their spending for such favors? No. In light of this, it is important to understand that simply saying "get the money out of politics" does not work if you are truly interested in fair elections.

Pushing to get money out of politics only works to the advantage of those already at the helm of the Swamp. They use the public outcry against money in politics to create complicated campaign finance regulations that require aspiring candidates or policy activists to hire expensive consultants to navigate the regulations and keep them on the right side of campaign finance law. This means the aspiring candidates or policy activists need to raise even more money to make their case or divert precious time from advocacy to administrative activities. Spending caps and burdensome filing requirements make it difficult for political outsiders to make a dent in the Swamp.

There will always be Swamp tactics as long as there is politics, but there is a price for such tactics. The price is the loss of respect for our system of government. Recent elections have shown that the bill for this price has now come due. Voters are tired of Swamp politics on both sides of the political aisle.

If taking the money out of politics is impractical, what then can we do to overcome the Swamp? Understand how it works. We must understand all of the control levers in the various government processes. We need to learn how to use such levers in a way that puts the people back in charge. In other words, the best way to battle the Swamp is with an informed electorate (that's you). So let's look at some of the tactics that can be used.

# 10

# COMMON TACTICS

As Jesus said, "No one can serve two masters. Either he will hate the one and love the other, or he will be devoted to the one and despise the other. You cannot serve both God and money" (Matt. 6:24). In the case of serving in elected office, one can either serve the best interests of the public or the best interests of the Swamp. Our system of government was designed to promote the general welfare of all of our citizens, not serve the needs of a self-anointed nobility. We have forgotten how our government is intended to work. The Swamp advocates have taken advantage of this lapse in memory.

How can we fill the memory gap? Refresh our memory on how our system of government was intended to work. Whenever Engineers design something, they invariably provide an operations manual to supplement the design specifications. If a user follows the operations manual, the system will work fine. If you throw out the operations manual and make it up as you go, the system is often used in ways for which it was not intended. The Founders created an operations manual for our system of government. It is called the Constitution.

The United States Constitution clearly designates what the federal government is authorized to do and is prohibited from doing. It even includes a limited number of provisions related to the operations of state governments. The state constitutions provide additional rules related to the operations of state governments. State legislators take oaths to support both the US Constitution and their respective state constitution.

As with any system, be it an aircraft or a system of government, operations manuals guide users through each part in the system, explaining how it is intended to work. For the purpose of this illustration, I have provided a list of intended operations and unintended operations for all of the basic processes found in our system of government. I've associated the *intended* operations with public servants simply executing their oaths of office. Conversely, I've associated the *unintended* operations with those who prefer to promote the priorities of the Swamp.

The following list is not comprehensive but is an attempt to highlight most of the tactics which I have observed during my relatively brief political life. It should be noted that I do not believe that any elected official is completely innocent of ever participating in a swamp tactic. In much the same way that we are all sinners and have fallen short of the glory of God, I submit that all elected officials have been tainted in some way by Swamp politics. It comes down to a matter of proportion. For public servants, the use of Swamp tactics is the exception not the rule. For Swamp servants, the use of Swamp tactics is the rule not the exception.

### General Election Tactics

My Grandpa Grybb used to tell me, "if you can't be the best, be the next best." I have found that advice to work well in most facets of life, except politics. The principle goal in any election is to get the most votes.

The overall goal of receiving the most votes can be achieved by accomplishing three basic objectives. The first objective is to make sure that all potential voters recognize your name. The second objective is to ensure that you leave people with a favorable impression of your name. The third objective is to ensure that the impression that you leave voters is better than the impression they have your opponent.

How one accomplishes these objectives is more art than science and varies for each individual. I have run for office twice. The first time, I came out of nowhere to defeat four former state representatives. The second time, I ran as an incumbent office holder with a track record that earned me national attention from the Democratic Party. Thankfully, I was successful in both campaigns by using tactics that I believe were consistent with those of a public servant not a servant of the Swamp.

### Public Servant

Campaigns can be very emotional journeys. After all, elections are a referendum on whether or not the majority of your fellow citizens like you better or your opponent. As such, it can get quite personal. Don't lose your soul in search of victory. There are a lot of distractions during a campaign. During one of my campaigns, one of my opponent's brothers offered to campaign for me. I turned him down. Family bonds are more important than political campaigns. The best way to navigate through campaign distractions is to keep your hands and feet in the ride at all times and focus on what is noble and true. Where God guides, He truly does provide.

There are many noble and true tactics used by public servants to win elections. I could easily devote an entire book to just this topic. Instead I have provided simply a primer on tactics one should consider if one would like to retain their integrity while running for office in Table 7.

## TABLE 7: PUBLIC SERVANT ELECTION TACTICS

| TACTIC | DESCRIPTION | ASSETS | EFFORT | COST | IMPACT |
|---|---|---|---|---|---|
| Canvassing (knocking on doors) | Knock on doors within your district and introduce yourself to prospective voters. | Comfortable shoes Walking list Campaign literature (essential to name recognition) | High | Low | High |
| Community events | Introduce yourself to residents of district at community events. | Community Calendar campaign literature | Low | Low-Medium | Medium |
| Social media | Create and make regular posts (daily is best) to social media accounts (e.g. Facebook, LinkedIn, Twitter, Instagram). This is free but posts can be promoted for nominal fee. | Social media accounts | Low-Medium | Low | Medium |

| TACTIC | DESCRIPTION | ASSETS | EFFORT | COST | IMPACT |
|--------|-------------|--------|--------|------|--------|
| Road rallies | Gather a group of volunteers to stand on corners of busy intersections during rush hour to smile and wave signs. | Volunteers | Low | Low | Medium |
| Letters to editors | Write editorials to local newspapers. | Relationships | Low | Free | Low-Medium |
| Endorsements | Seek the endorsements of prominent individuals in your community or someone who would be recognized favorably in your community. | Relationships | Low | Low | Medium-High |
| Dialing for dollars | Call everyone you know to ask for donations then call everyone who has donated to anyone in your party in the past. | Donor list | High | Low | Medium |

| TACTIC | DESCRIPTION | ASSETS | EFFORT | COST | IMPACT |
|---|---|---|---|---|---|
| Mailers | Prepare a compelling letter asking for donations. Include easy methods for recipients to submit donations. | Donor list Letter | Low | Medium | Low |
| Online Fund-raising | Create a website that accepts online donations. Promote "moneybombs" to reach specific fund-raising targets. | Website | Medium | Medium | Medium |
| Professional fund-raising | Hire a professional fund-raiser either on commission or via retainer agreement. | None | Medium | Medium-High | Low-High |
| Talk radio | Arrange for interviews with radio show hosts with shows that air in your district. | None | Low | Free | Medium |
| Press releases | Issue press releases to media contacts covering your district regarding events or important announcements. | Media list | Low | Free | Medium |

| TACTIC | DESCRIPTION | ASSETS | EFFORT | COST | IMPACT |
|---|---|---|---|---|---|
| Earned media | Stage events or announcements that would peak the interest of media. | Varies | Varies | Varies | Low–High |
| Poll-sitting | Staff polling areas with volunteers promoting your name via signs or literature. | Signs Literature | Medium | Low | Low |
| Website | Create a campaign website featuring bio, platform, events, contact information, and the ability to accept donations. Most websites feature static content or dynamic content which is automatically posted from another source. | Platform Campaign calendar Bank account PO Box | Low | Medium | High |
| Yard signs | Create and post signs that highlight your name, office, and means of finding more information (e.g. website). | Graphic | Low | Low | Low |
| Bumper stickers | Produce stickers with your name on them. | Graphic | Low | Low | Low |
| Opposition Research | Research opponent in support of contrast-based marketing materials and overall campaign strategy. | Varies | Low | Low | Medium |

| TACTIC | DESCRIPTION | ASSETS | EFFORT | COST | IMPACT |
|---|---|---|---|---|---|
| Robo calls | Record short messages by your or a surrogate. | Call list, Robo call service | Low | Low | Low |
| Mailers | Mail campaign literature to prospective voters. | Voter list, Graphic design, Printer, Mailer | Low | High | Medium |
| Absentee Voter (AV) Chase | Mail campaign literature to absentee voters on the same date they receive their absentee ballot. | Absentee voter list, Graphic design, Printer, AV chase service | Low | High | High |
| Newspaper advertising | Create an ad in local newspaper or community pamphlets. | Graphic design | Low | Medium | Low |
| Radio ads | Create radio ads to play on local radio stations. | Script, Audio recording | Low | Medium | Medium |
| TV ads | Create TV ads to play on local TV stations. | Script, Film crew, Video recording | Medium | High | Medium* |

* High prestige points, but less effective during the age of DVRs.

In order to be successful, I recommend that you have the following assets at the ready before committing to run:

- Family support
- Prayer support
- Campaign Team
- Campaign Plan
- Financial Plan
- Platform
- Voter lists
- Good health

I used basically the same tactics in my primaries and general elections. The big difference between primaries and general elections is the involvement of the respective political party organizations. Typically, the parties will stay neutral during primaries although this is not always the case. It was not the case in my first primary election. I was new to the political arena and many Republican activists preferred a "known quantity." They introduced their preferred candidate at the eleventh hour and provided commensurate financial backing to this candidate in exchange for agreeing to run. We won anyway, and I am happy to say that many of my former detractors are now ardent supporters because I ran a positive campaign.

In general elections, the state party will typically deploy additional resources only if a candidate is facing a tight race. Campaign funds are precious. While candidates are focused on their individual races, state parties are focused on ensuring victories in statewide elections to gain majorities in the House and Senate in order to control state policy direction. They need to look at the entire portfolio of races and determine which races would benefit from financial support and for which races extra money would have a negligible effect. This is one of the reasons that state parties prefer candidates who can self-finance. The state party and many other campaign funding sources are hesitant to allocate precious financial resources to any race unless it is within a 5 percent margin of victory. Inside of 5 percent, you will likely get additional funding. Outside of 5 percent, you will not get additional funding. Additional funding can only move the needle so far, though. There is no substitute for a solid candidate in a competitive district.

Beyond the potential for direct party funding, what can you expect from your political party during the general election? One should not expect direct contributions to candidate committees. The party typically prefers to retain control of party funds. The preferred method of support for a given party's candidate is with mailers or ads produced and distributed by the state party directly or via friendly third-party organizations. If direct contributions are provided to the candidate, these contributions are typically provided as "gift-in-kind" contributions so the party can retain control over content.

Parties will also assist candidates with Election Day Operations (EDO). Such operations include Get Out the Vote (GOTV) activities, such as phone banks or party canvassers. Other valuable services provided by the party include providing poll challengers or watchers and legal support should there be any election fraud or legal challenges such as a recount. Parties also provide appointees to boards of canvassers throughout the state that are responsible for monitoring and certifying election results.

### *Swamp Servant*

My mentor in the Senate, Senator John Pappageorge, always had a simple way of explaining what could sometimes be complex concepts. One of his favorite diagrams regarding campaign messaging (depicted in Figure 6) provides a good distinction between the election tactics of a public servant and those of a Swamp servant.

Public servants only share what is true. Swamp servants often set up shop on the other side of the diagram. Public servants can, and often do, produce "compare and contrast" ads that may reflect negatively on their opponents. Just because an ad reflects negatively on a candidate, however, does not mean it is not true. Where things get dicey is when an opponent makes assertions about *why* the candidate voted the way that they did. That is impossible to know unless the candidate is on record with such assertions.

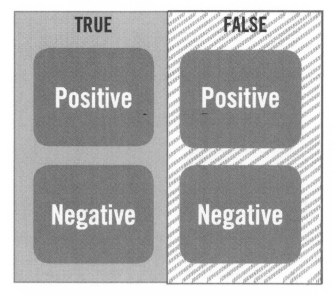

*Figure 6 Types of Messaging*

Conversely, just because an opponent claims a certain position on an issue, does not mean that that position is true. Swamp servants can run a 100 percent positive campaign that is full of lies. In essence, a Swamp candidate can run as someone they are not if they have enough money and hutzpah to sell it to voters. More often than not, however, Swamp candidates simply throw dirt at their opponent until they find something that sticks with voters. The first time that I ran for office, the Democrats did not have any negative messages that were true, so they told voters incessantly via TV ads that I would take away Social Security and Medicare—as a state senator. Not only would I never *do* that, I never *said* that I would do that. That did not stop my opponent from making such claims in an attempt to scare what is typically the most reliable voting block in an election: seniors.

To better understand Swamp servant tactics, read the comprehensive list in Table 8.

# TABLE 8: SWAMP SERVANT ELECTION TACTICS

| TACTIC | DESCRIPTION | COMMENTARY |
|---|---|---|
| Run as someone they're not | Pander to key voting blocks. Use money to rebrand a candidate and hide true public service and private sector record. Run an insider as an outsider. | We are a Center-Right nation. Even hard-core liberals tend to voice conservative policy positions during elections. |
| Dig for dirt | No one is perfect. As Stalin's Chief of Police once said, "Show me the man and I will find the crime." Even the most principled candidate will have flaws that can be exploited with enough resources and marketing prowess. In order to assist in the identification of these flaws, the Freedom of Information Act (FOIA) process is often used to go on "fishing expeditions" looking for an indiscreet communication or expression that can be exploited (often out of context) on the campaign trail. | On the campaign trail, I was being followed by a gentleman by the name of Daniel Bloomberg working on behalf of a progressive organization called American Bridge. Daniel would routinely sit politely at the back of the room and videotape everything that I said. Kind of creepy in a Truman Show kind of way, but, since I don't change my message based on the audience, I am not worried about consistency. The stated mission of American Bridge is to "hold Republicans accountable." |
| Tamper with recorded media | The technology now exists to modify photographs, audio recordings, and video recordings to suit any message the perpetrator seeks to convey. | One of the most egregious uses of this tactic involved Michigan Supreme Court Justice Cliff Taylor's 2008 re-election campaign. Democrats took frame-by-frame video footage of the justice during a hearing and isolated a photo where his eyes were closed due to blinking. They then ran a series of ads referring to him as the "sleeping judge." |

| TACTIC | DESCRIPTION | COMMENTARY |
|---|---|---|
| Paid agitators | Campaigns can hire "trolls" to slander candidates on social media often using fake or non-specific names to hide their identity. | Most social media platforms include the ability to block slanderous trolls. I have no problem with people who disagree with me airing their discontent. I do have a problem handing over the microphone that connects to a social media audience that I built over to someone intent upon spreading misinformation as a means of draining precious time and financial resources from my campaign to refute such accusations. |
| Public assets | Unscrupulous campaigns will use public assets such as paid staff or email lists to support campaign activities they would otherwise have to pay for out of their campaign budgets. | The Democratic opponent in my 2014 re-election campaign was caught using the school email list to promote her campaign. It was the third time that she was caught doing so. Each time she was caught, she issued an apology and said it wouldn't happen again. I didn't have the resources to pursue legal action. |
| Fake news | There is a blatant political bias in many of the news stories promoted by many media outlets. In many respects, these outlets can be viewed as marketing agencies for their preferred political party (most often Democrats). Their "news" stories often feature the messaging that can be found in their preferred party's campaign literature, effectively giving them free advertising. | Fake news is not limited to national outlets. When the Michigan Senate passed legislation to require CPL holders to carry "concealed" rather than "open" in so-called gun-free zones such as schools, many newspaper headlines read "Senate OK's guns in schools." The natural assumption by many readers of these headlines was that the Senate was now allowing people to carry guns into schools when they couldn't do so before when in fact the legislation only changed the manner in which weapons were to be carried. |

| TACTIC | DESCRIPTION | COMMENTARY |
| --- | --- | --- |
| Media censorship | Media outlets do not need to promote "fake news" in order to shape the outcomes of elections. Executives and editors in media outlets choose what stories are printed or aired and which are not. This censorship can sometimes keep readers or listeners from hearing important truths about a given policy issue that might shape their views. | In June 2015, I submitted an editorial to my local newspaper that highlighted how a local school district added fifteen administrators over a time period that student enrollment was down. Despite providing evidence of such malfeasance, the paper refused to post the editorial after it received protests from liberal activists on the school board seeking additional school funding. |
| Editorial smears | The reputation of an elected official is one of their most valuable assets. Media pundits know this. Sadly, many pundits in the media target this asset and spew all sorts of accusations whether true or not because as public figures elected officials are not able to charge someone with slander. | It is very difficult to fight organizations that buy ink by the barrel. |
| Lie about opponents | When all else fails, unscrupulous campaigns will simply lie about their opponent if they think it will impact the election results favorably. | During my first campaign for office, the Democrats launched a massive marketing campaign to falsely claim that I would eliminate Social Security and Medicare. |

Swamps are murky. Many of the tactics of Swamp denizens are likewise rather murky. The good news is that they often dissolve in the bright light of truth. The bad news is that spotlights often cost quite a bit of money. If you would like a more comprehensive view of Swamp politics, I recommend reading *Rules for Radicals Defeated: A Practical Guide for Defeating Obama/Alinsky* by Jeff Hedgpeth.

### Leadership Election Tactics

As noted in chapter 8, the first and most important vote that any senator makes upon election to office is that of Senate majority leader. The same could be said of Representatives regarding the Speaker of the House. These leadership positions are determined by a vote of the members elected to each chamber. The one with the most votes from their respective caucus wins the position.

As discussed earlier, I was successful during my first campaign for a leadership position that no one else campaigned for—assistant caucus chair. The duration of my campaign for that position lasted about five seconds, until Senator Pappageorge closed all nominations. Leading up to my second term of office, I cast my hat into the ring for Senate majority leader. The extent of my campaign effort was pretty much limited to printing out business cards for my Principled Leadership Fund. I simply wished to give my colleagues an alternative. Going into the election, Senator Meekhof had already wrapped up a critical mass of commitments from my colleagues via committee assignment, leadership position, or financial commitments.

Needless to say, he won the election as our Senate Majority Leader. I even voted for him as a sign of unity. This just goes to show you that it is very difficult for even the most principled elected officials to have a perfect voting record.

### *Public Servant*

Throughout my first campaign for the Senate, even before I was elected, candidates, or their surrogates, who were seeking Senate leadership positions courted my vote. I had a simple question. What was your action plan for fixing our state? After all, I was running to help implement policies that would fix our state. I assumed that being a leader meant that the person who assumed the position would *lead* the state policy discussions. I wanted to know in which direction they would lead. In light of the power to control public policy inherent in the position, I believe that it is *very* important to understand the policy positions of a prospective leader.

It is also important for leadership elections to align with the policy sentiments of the respective party's grass roots. In other words, leadership's policy views should align with the party platform. There are both practical and philosophical reasons for this assertion. The practical reason is that strong grassroots support typically translates into strong support for caucus members in their next election. The philosophical reason is that most would be led to believe that a Republican majority should generally promote policies that align with the Republican platform while a Democrat majority should generally promote policies that align with the Democratic platform. After all, it is the grass roots within the respective parties who determine during state and national party conventions what their platforms contain. When a Republican majority promotes legislation that lines up better with the Democratic platform than Republican platform or vice versa, the party grass roots have a right to be upset.

# TABLE 9: PUBLIC SERVANT LEADERSHIP ELECTION TACTICS

| TACTIC | DESCRIPTION | COMMENTARY |
|---|---|---|
| Party Platform | The prospective leader commits to promoting policies that implement the platform of the respective party. | One example of this tactic would be a prospective Republican leader committing to repeal Obamacare |
| Principled Leadership | The prospective leader commits to promoting policies that adhere to a set of well-defined principles that may or may not align 100 percent with the pertinent party platform. | One example of this tactic would be a prospective leader committing not to raise taxes |
| Charisma | The prospective leader is a "larger than life" natural leader that attracts a broad base of support. | Examples of such figures would be high profile military officers or media personalities |
| Grassroots Support | The prospective leader has built a strong base of support in the grassroots members of the respective party | Leaders that are regular speakers at grassroots events or earn a great deal of respect from grassroots activists at conventions does not necessarily translate into being respected by fellow members of a caucus. Sadly, it is often a contrarian indicator. |

| TACTIC | DESCRIPTION | COMMENTARY |
|---|---|---|
| Relationships | The prospective leader builds trusting relationships with prospective caucus members. | Social networking is very effective in leadership races. These networks can be built via shared experience serving in another capacity, longtime friendships, or hosting regular get-togethers such as weekly BBQ's |
| Merit-based Committee Broker | The prospective leader assigns committee chairmanships on the basis of the experience and aptitude of members. | One example of this tactic would be assigning a civil engineer to oversee the transportation budget |

As it turns out, policy positions and grassroots support often have very little to do with leadership elections. While there are indeed exceptions, more often than not, leadership elections are determined almost exclusively by Swamp tactics.

### Swamp Servant

To the victors go the spoils. In the case of Michigan, the spoils equate to control of a $56 billion per year state budget which can be used by the leader of each legislative chamber to reward friends and destroy enemies. In addition to taxpayer resources, leadership also often has oversight of millions of dollars in campaign-related funds that can be used to reward friends and destroy enemies. Is it any wonder why temptations of this magnitude tend to result in "ends justify the means" campaigns when it comes to leadership races? A sample of some of the Swamp tactics used to secure leadership positions can be found in Table 10.

## TABLE 10: SWAMP SERVANT LEADERSHIP ELECTION TACTICS

| TACTIC | DESCRIPTION | COMMENTARY |
|---|---|---|
| Daddy Warbucks | The prospective leader offers cash from personal fortunes or leadership funds which they control. | Candidates who are not able to self-finance their campaigns are most susceptible to this tactic. Offers of significant campaign contributions are typically held back or "teased" until a candidate is desperate for funds and therefore amenable to making a commitment for the leadership race. |
| Caucus campaign committee control | As a Michigan state senator, I am expected to contribute $7,000 per year to our Senate Republican Campaign Committee to assist in the elections of fellow members and retain a majority in the Michigan Senate. In addition to these dues, these committees often raise a significant amount of money from lobbyists and party faithful. Prospective chamber leaders often opt to control the purse strings. The goal being to ensure that candidates who support the leader are elected and those who don't are hamstrung. | Similar to the Daddy Warbucks tactic except that the prospective leader uses "other people's money." |
| The Landlord | The prospective leader purchases or leases property close to the Capitol and leases or subleases rooms at below-market value to members who live a long distance from the Capitol. | As you might imagine, it would be difficult to make a decision that would risk losing a low-rent domicile near the Capitol. |

| TACTIC | DESCRIPTION | COMMENTARY |
|---|---|---|
| Committee broker | The prospective leader offers a committee chairmanship to a member in exchange for the member's leadership vote. | Not all committee chairs are created equal. Fund-raising can be made exceptionally easier as a committee chair. For example, the Insurance and Health Committees are highly desirable because the insurance companies and hospitals are often very generous with campaign contributions. |
| Leadership position broker | Like the committee broker, prospective leaders will offer specific non-chair leadership positions to members in exchange for their leadership votes, thus building a slate of friendly members for other leadership positions. | Many leadership positions result in additional direct compensation. For example, the MI Senate Majority Leader receives a $23,400 supplement to their salary while the Appropriations Chair receives an additional $6,300.* |
| Staff "volunteers" | Funds are not the only resources over which a prospective leader has influence. Prospective chamber leaders can also encourage staff to help canvass for friendly candidates. | In Michigan, staff members have very generous vacation allotments on the order of four weeks or more per year. In exchange for this vacation, staffers are expected to "volunteer" staff days to assist in campaigns for candidates in their respective parties. |

* SOURCE: Salaries and Expense Allowances for Positions Subject to SOCC Recommendations, Michigan.gov, https://www.michigan.gov/documents/mdcs/2011SalariesExpAllowances_342262_7.pdf

Leadership campaigns often result in campaigns within the campaigns as various leadership candidates provide various levels of support to candidates likely to support them during the general election, which precedes the leadership election. Promises of all sorts are made along the way. Sometimes they are even kept.

### Legislative Tactics

The principle role of legislators is to propose, evaluate, and enact legislation necessary to promote the common good. After all, the word *legislator* is derived from the word *legislation*. Legislation can be proposed in many ways. Lobbyists acting on behalf of their clients are typically the most prolific sources of legislation. Party platforms serve as another source of legislation. Candidate platforms are another source of legislation as elected officials seek to make good on their campaign promises. Headlines of the day drive more than their fair share of legislation—sometimes to promote the best interests of the common good, but many times in the interest of self-promotion.

My favorite source of legislative ideas is from constituents. One of my favorite examples of a bill sparking from an inquiry by constituents dates back to a meeting that I had in 2015 with Boy Scout Troop 743. As I often do after introducing myself and quizzing the scouts on civics, I opened the floor to questions. Scouts Kevin Kapanowski and Will Cothron asked me why the school they attended no longer allowed bake sales. The proceeds from these bake sales were used to fund educational field trips that the students truly enjoyed. No funds, no field trips. They were told it was due to a decision made by the state. After some investigation, my Senate team found that there was indeed a prohibition on bake sales due to a rule promulgated by the Michigan Department of Education (MDE) in response to a Federal Law promoted by Michelle Obama. Her legislation placed restrictions on "non-compliant" fund-raisers that schools may have on school property as part of her Smart Snacks initiative. MDE chose to allow zero "non-compliant" fund-raisers, effectively shutting down bake sales at schools throughout Michigan. When I found this out, I introduced legislation to overrule MDE's decision and allow so-called "non-compliant" fund-raisers at the schools. The scouts testified in favor of the legislation, as did my good friend Lori Levi whose kids attended the same Canton Charter Academy attended by the boys. Lori brought samples of the foods into our committee hearings that were both "compliant" and "non-compliant" as determined by the federal government's Smart Snack list. Some bagels were on the list. Some were not. Some Pop Tarts were on the list. Some were not. The distinctions seemed to be arbitrary and not related to any consistent nutritional guidelines. My legislation was eventually signed into law by Governor Snyder but not before Will and Kevin had an opportunity to tell their story to a national audience on *Fox and Friends*. They rocked it.

It has been estimated that it costs taxpayers five thousand dollars for every bill that is introduced. In light of this, legislation should not be introduced for frivolous pursuits. The power invested in legislators to legislate is a serious responsibility that requires principled deliberation.

### Public Servant

The legislative tactics employed by a public servant are focused on determining whether or not a given bill is in the best interest of the citizens. A sample list of tactics used by public servants to evaluate whether or not to support a bill is provided in Table 11.

## TABLE II: PUBLIC SERVANT LEGISLATIVE TACTICS

| TACTIC | DESCRIPTION | COMMENTARY |
|---|---|---|
| Merit | Sponsor promotes the legislation on the basis of its merit. It follows the principle that one should win the argument before winning the vote. | Such was my attempt when it came to providing a means of fixing Michigan's roads without increasing taxes. I failed in my attempt, despite a compelling business case for my proposed solution. |
| Party Platform | Sponsor promotes legislation on the basis of its alignment with a particular plank of a given party's platform. | In 2013, I was ashamed that our Republican-controlled legislative bodies and governor were pursuing the expansion of Medicaid in accordance with Section 2001 of HR 3590 (aka Obamacare). This policy clearly violated the Republican platform, which promoted the repeal of Obamacare. In response to this legislation, I introduced legislation that would provide access to care for the expansion population without expanding Medicaid. Despite the introduction of my legislation, the Republican-controlled legislature and governor chose to expand Obamacare in Michigan. (This legislation is now poised for automatic repeal because it will not yield the projected savings.) |

| TACTIC | DESCRIPTION | COMMENTARY |
|---|---|---|
| Candidate Platform | Almost every candidate has a set of policy goals they promise to enact when in office. It is laudable that legislators follow through on the promises they made to their constituents during their campaign for office. | I created the Vote Compass to keep me consistent with the principles captured in my campaign literature. It has helped me earn the distinction of consistently being rated Michigan's most conservative Senator. |
| Constitutional | Every elected official takes an oath to support the Constitution. That means they are obligated to ensure that every piece of legislation is constitutional before they vote to support it. | Regrettably, there are some legislators who have ceded the responsibility of determining whether or not a piece of legislation is constitutional to the courts. If that were the appropriate course of action, then why do legislators swear an oath of office that requires them to support the Constitution? |

| TACTIC | DESCRIPTION | COMMENTARY |
|---|---|---|
| Needle Mover | Sometimes a given piece of legislation may not achieve the end goal of a given policy position but it "moves the needle" towards that end. | During my push to end Common Core in Michigan, several grassroots activists provided me with legislation that would not only repeal Common Core but would also effectively end Federal control of education in Michigan due to its inclusion of a provision related to Federal funding ties. While I do not believe the Federal government has any role in education per Article I Section 8 of the US Constitution, I knew that if the legislation contained that provision it would be vetoed by the governor because it would put billions in Federal funding at risk. I proposed a substitute that removed this provision but retained the provisions that would repeal Common Core. In other words, the bill would move the needle towards less federal involvement although it did not completely remove their influence over education in the state. |
| Tough Vote | Elected officials are convinced that the only way to effectively fix a serious problem is to vote for a bill that will upset a significant block of constituents. | There are times when a problem is kicked down the road for so many years that it leads to a crisis that must finally be addressed even though it might upset key constituencies. |

| TACTIC | DESCRIPTION | COMMENTARY |
|---|---|---|
| Co-Sponsors | One way of determining support for legislation before it is formally introduced is to solicit co-sponsors from legislative colleagues. If a majority of colleagues sponsor the legislation, it bodes well for passage of the bill. | In the Michigan Senate, there are thirty-eight Senators. If I can get at least twenty Senators to co-sponsor a bill, it is highly likely it will pass. |
| Double Bluebacks | If one anticipates resistance in one legislative body or the other, it is often wise to introduce the same bill in both the House and the Senate by requesting what are called Double Bluebacks in the Michigan legislature. The version that moves the furthest the fastest would be promoted as the version to ultimately be supported. | My good friend, former State Representative Tom Hooker, and I both introduced Choose Life License Plate legislation agreeing that whichever version was voted out of its respective chamber first would be the version supported by both of us. |
| Work Group or Commission Findings | Some policy issues are so complex that they warrant the establishment of a work group or commission to evaluate the problem and propose solutions before a bill or bill package is introduced. | As a result of my service on Michigan's Criminal Justice Policy Commission, I developed legislation to govern the development and operation of a Criminal Justice Data Management System that would integrate state and county criminal data systems. There were sixteen state agencies and eighty-three counties with quite a variety of data systems. |

## TACTIC

Immediate Effect

## DESCRIPTION

Unless the legislature adopts what is referred to as Immediate Effect for a given bill, the bill will not become law until after the legislative session is over.

## COMMENTARY

According to the Michigan Constitution, Immediate Effect requires the approval of two-thirds of the legislators in each body. Failure to designate Immediate Effect means that the legislation will not go into effect until ninety days after Sine Die, which is the last official day of each legislative session.

In the final analysis, the legislative tactics pursued by an advocate of public servant tactics promote a transparent, deliberative process for passing legislation. We will now look at some different approaches to passing legislation favored by the denizens of the Swamp.

### Swamp Servant

In contrast to the legislative practices of public servants, the tactics of Swamp servants are often murky and devoid of transparency. It is my hope that the exposure of some of these tactics will help voters better understand how good legislation rots in committee while bad legislation seems to get the fast track at times. Some of the more common examples of Swamp sausage–making tactics can be found in Table 12.

## TABLE 12: SWAMP SERVANT LEGISLATIVE TACTICS

| TACTIC | DESCRIPTION | COMMENTARY |
|---|---|---|
| Special Interest Push | The vast majority of legislation is written not by legislators or their staff. It is written by special interest groups. The subject matter expertise of these groups can at times be valuable, but more often than not, their legislation is intended to provide some sort of advantage for their particular special interest often to the detriment of broader public interests. Furthermore, special interests are typically tied to Political Action Committees (PACs), which can provide significant financial contributions to candidates and various campaign funds. | I once asked a prominent member of our Senate leadership team for a floor vote on a bill that I had sponsored. In response to my request, I was asked which special interest group was supporting the legislation? The question took me aback. No special interest was pushing my legislation. I was pushing the legislation on behalf of my constituents, and frankly on behalf of all of the residents of our state. After all, our job is to serve as representatives of the citizens of Michigan. Why would I be asked which special interest group was backing the legislation unless that was the primary determinant as to whether or not it would get a vote? |

| TACTIC | DESCRIPTION | COMMENTARY |
|---|---|---|
| Overton Window | Cast dispersion upon any solution that does not fit within a political orthodoxy that benefits the bill sponsor(s). Sometimes masquerades as a "tough choice" vote when in reality there are other choices. These other choices are typically not beneficial to the bill sponsor(s) or are simply so innovative that they challenge the orthodoxy of colleagues to such an extent that they revert back to their orthodoxy. | Michigan's roads do not have reputation as the best roads in the nation to put it lightly. A task force report stated that a minimum of $1.2 billion of additional funding was required to fix the roads. When legislation was drafted to implement the findings of the task force, it proposed to increase taxes by over $2 billion. The governor, Senate majority leader, Speaker, and every media outlet insisted that we needed to increase taxes to fix the roads. Yet I found a way to fix the roads without raising taxes that never made it into the Overton Window painted by the media, the governor, and others. In my frustration, I challenged them all to a debate. Not one of the leading advocates of the tax increase accepted the challenge. |

| TACTIC | DESCRIPTION | COMMENTARY |
|---|---|---|
| Show Vote | A show vote is when leadership puts a bill intended to convey support for a given policy issue but in fact enables the enactment of legislation that does the exact opposite. | Probably the best example of a show vote pertains to Obamacare. The Republican-controlled House voted fifty-four times to repeal Obamacare while Barack Obama was president. Republicans gained control of the Senate on the heels of promises to repeal Obamacare. Yet these same legislators could not muster the votes to Repeal Obamacare once Republican Donald Trump had assumed the Oval Office. |
| The Naughty List | One of the ways a chamber leader can penalize a caucus member who fails to follow their whims (i.e. kiss their pinky ring) is to put them on the "naughty list." The naughty list refers to individuals whose legislation is not supposed to get a vote in committee, or, if it manages to get reported out of committee, will not get a vote on the floor. The naughty list can also be a factor in negotiations with the leader of the other chamber or governor. Committee chairs can also have a naughty list that will effectively trap otherwise good bills in their committee. | In the wake of reading George Orwell's *1984* for the first time and witnessing "shout downs" at my Alma Mater, I introduced legislation to defend campus free speech. The chair of the Senate Judiciary Committee told me that the Senate majority leader did not want it to move. Sensing my obvious frustration, he added "but we can talk if you get the ACLU to support it." After some tweaks, I had a bill that earned the support of the ACLU and the Goldwater Institute. In other words, it had broad-based support. Despite this, the bill still resides in his committee. |

## TACTIC

The Nice List

## DESCRIPTION

One of the ways a chamber leader can reward a caucus member who does them a "favor" is to put them on the "nice list." The nice list refers to individuals whose legislation will get preferential treatment in committee on the chamber floor. The nice list can also be a factor in negotiations with the leader of the other chamber or governor effectively prioritizing the passage of legislation by list members. Committee chairs can also have a nice list that will effectively enable bills to be reported from their committee regardless of their merit.

## COMMENTARY

The same Senator who did the bidding of the Senate majority leader (SML) and buried my Campus Free Speech bill in his committee has apparently earned significant brownie points from the SML, resulting in a virtual rubber stamp for all of his legislation. Blind obedience has its perks.

## TACTIC

Headline Chasers

## DESCRIPTION

Tragic events often result in the introduction of legislation designed more to promote the sponsor than to actually address the root cause of the tragedy in a manner that is reasonable and fair. It is often introduced in response to public cries to "Just do something." Too many elected officials adhere to the Rahm Emmanuel doctrine of "Don't let a crisis go to waste."

## COMMENTARY

In summer 2014, a soccer referee was punched in the head by a player during a soccer match in my hometown resulting in his subsequent death. Capitalizing on the headlines associated with this tragedy, one of my colleagues introduced legislation to increase the criminal penalties for assaulting a referee, thus elevating the status of a referee. I made the argument that assault is assault regardless of who was assaulted. Furthermore, Article 1 Section 2 guaranteed equal protection under the law for all citizens. In light of this, and with the referee's widow in the audience, I was obligated by my oath of office to make a heart wrenching no vote on the legislation.

## DESCRIPTION

The leaders of each chamber enter negotiations over each chamber's legislative agenda with a list of "caucus priorities." They keep score as to how many bills in their respective chamber are moving in the other chamber. If progress is not commensurate with expectations, the processing of bills from the offending chamber is slowed or halted altogether until the desired progress is achieved. The merit of the pertinent legislation from a citizens perspective is not typically a factor in such discussions.

## COMMENTARY

This process is often complicated by fights over whether or not it is a House or Senate member who would get credit for the official Public Act on popular legislation that would play well in campaign literature.

## TACTIC

Horse Trading

## TACTIC

Create a Crisis

## DESCRIPTION

Just because a crisis doesn't present itself does not mean that policy makers are not able to create a crisis if it meant that it could be used to justify a policy move they would like to make.

## COMMENTARY

Health care is a prime example of an industry where government interference in the free market has created a crisis that some in government would like to use as justification for even more control of our lives. Government mandates and other regulations have been driving up the cost of health care since the 1960's. Obamacare was introduced with the promise that it would lower the cost of quality insurance for everyone. Instead, it created a crisis in which people pay more for less coverage. The elected officials responsible for this debacle are now calling for even more control over our lives via a single payer health-care system which some believe was the end game all along.

## TACTIC

Keyword Legislation

## DESCRIPTION

Certain keywords in legislation often make opposition to this legislation politically dangerous. Regardless of the merit of the specific provisions of the legislation, this legislation is often viewed in the media through the lens of such keywords rather than the merit of the specific legislation making no votes problematic considering the context for the no votes is rarely provided. Voting against such legislation will typically show up as a black mark on your record during campaigns that will often require expensive explanations.

## COMMENTARY

In Michigan, there is a significant opioid abuse problem. Some legislators teamed up to introduce legislation to address the issue that not only was ineffective at preventing the proliferation of opioids in our communities, it also introduced additional bureaucracy into the doctor-patient relationship. This bureaucracy would continue the march of doctor-patient visits down the path towards the same useless avalanche of paperwork required at a mortgage closing. The legislation would increase the cost of health care without getting to the root cause of the problem. Opposition to the legislation is likely to be cast in subsequent campaign lit as "support of opioid abuse."

| TACTIC | DESCRIPTION | COMMENTARY |
|---|---|---|
| Bait and Switch | Lawmakers will make the case for passing a given law based on one purpose (typically a popular one) while actually doing so with another purpose in mind (typically an unpopular one). | A prime example of this approach to setting policy pertains to Michigan's 2015 gas tax increase. Within two months of the citizens rejecting a $2 billion tax increase proposal by a four-to-one margin, the legislature introduced a different proposal to raise taxes by $600 million that did not require a vote of the people. Despite my vocal opposition, it passed. Shortly thereafter, a supplemental budget bill was passed that transferred $400 million in general fund revenue from the transportation budget to other budget priorities including backfilling holes in the Michigan Department of Health and Human Services budget created by the expansion of Medicaid. |
| Reaching Across the Aisle | Establishment leadership invested in preserving the status quo are often more likely to talk with members of the other party than they are to talk with members of their own party seeking to honor their commitments to voters. | Not all bi-partisan activities benefit citizens. In Senator Ted Cruz's book, *A Time for Truth*, he shares how Republican collusion with Democrats on a procedural vote would allow Democrats to increase the debt ceiling while allowing Republicans to vote no on the actual debt ceiling increase vote. |

| TACTIC | DESCRIPTION | COMMENTARY |
|---|---|---|
| Veto Threat | Chamber leadership can often take advantage of the special access to the governor they enjoy. As such, they can use the threat of a governor's veto to keep a bill from progressing out of committee or out of a given chamber. Sometimes the threat is true. Sometimes it is not. Either way it has the same effect unless the bill sponsor has direct access to the governor. | I believe that everyone in the legislative process needs to play positions and be accountable for how they perform in those positions. If a bill has sufficient support in both chambers to make it to the governor's desk, it should be placed upon the governor's desk. Governors need to be held accountable for their votes as much as the legislators. |
| Playing the Long Game | Term-limited officials often telegraph their future employment objectives by promoting legislation that would benefit these potential employers in some way. | The former House Appropriations Chair was appointed by the governor to the lucrative position of State Budget Director shortly after the end of his term. As House Appropriations Chair he was known to be a strong advocate for the governor's appropriation policies. |

## TACTIC

Lawfare

## DESCRIPTION

If a given party has difficulty winning enough elections to gain sufficient votes for their policy initiatives, they often resort to "lawfare." *Lawfare* is a term for when a group launches lawsuits in friendly courts in an attempt to legislate from the bench.

## COMMENTARY

*Roe v Wade* is a prime example of an attempt by abortion advocates to use the judiciary to effectively pass a law that did not have sufficient support via a legislative process. Article I Section I of the US Constitution states that "All legislative powers herein granted shall be vested in a Congress."

These tactics are not pretty. As frustrating as they may be to citizens at large, I can assure you that they are even more frustrating to many public servants who simply ran for office to serve the best interests of their constituents.

### Committee Tactics

The proceedings of a committee are governed by the committee chair in accordance with rules adopted at the beginning of each legislative term. Committees are intended to be forums of detailed deliberation on the pro's and con's of a given piece of legislation. Committee members hear testimony from supporters and detractors of bills. Upon hearing testimonies from policy advocates, it is the responsibility of committee members to ensure that any bill reported favorably from the committee has been thoroughly vetted and cleaned up in preparation for consideration by the entire legislative chamber.

### Public Servant

Public servants have three basic options when considering legislation before any committee upon which they serve: fix it, block it, or report it. A list of standard public servant committee tactics can be found in Table 13.

## TABLE 13: PUBLIC SERVANT COMMITTEE TACTICS

| TACTIC | DESCRIPTION | COMMENTARY |
| --- | --- | --- |
| Fix It | Words matter…especially in legislation that will likely need to be interpreted by citizens seeking to comply with the words of the legislation and judges seeking to rule in accordance with the words of the legislation. Committees should be places where misleading interpretations can be clarified and concerns raised in committee testimonies are addressed. | A good way to evaluate whether or not legislation needs "fixing" is to role play from the perspective of someone attempting to comply with the law or a judge attempting to rule in accordance with the law. |
| Block It | If a bill is unconstitutional or disagrees with key elements of an elected official's party platform or individual platform on which they ran, it is the duty of that official to oppose any favorable reporting of the bill from committee. | It can be difficult for some lawmakers to oppose legislation offered by members of their own party or with whom they have a good working relationship. It often comes down to a choice between relationships and principles. |

## COMMENTARY

A good practice of responsible committee chairs is to have at least two hearings on a given piece of legislation. During the first hearing, testimonials of supporters and detractors are heard. During the second hearing (often at least a week later), committee members are asked to vote on whether or not the bill should be reported from committee. This delay between testimony and voting can often be used to improve the legislation before it is introduced to the chamber floor for consideration.

## TACTIC    DESCRIPTION

Report It  If a bill is constitutional and agrees with a respective elected official's party platform or individual platform on which they ran, it is the duty of that official to support a favorable report of the bill from committee to the legislative chamber for further consideration.

Responsible committees will ensure that any legislation that comes before the committee will receive a thorough evaluation before it finds its way to the chamber floor. Colleagues need to have confidence that the product of any committee is a quality product.

### Swamp Servant

Swamp servants typically view the committee process as a temporary inconvenience that needs to be overcome in order to get to the goal of a roll call vote on the chamber floor. Conversely, the power of committee chairs to effectively block or report a bill lends itself to significant opportunities for mischief. A sample of swamp servant committee tactics can be found in Table 14.

# TABLE 14 SWAMP SERVANT COMMITTEE TACTICS

| TACTIC | DESCRIPTION | COMMENTARY |
|---|---|---|
| Vapor Trails | Vapor trails refer to the moisture that is seen humid air condenses near the wing tips of a fast moving aircraft. Legislation that is pushed through committee so fast that there is little or no deliberation is a disservice to the purpose of the committee process. | I have been on committees where over a dozen pieces of legislation were reviewed for the first time and reported out in about an hour. Granted, not all legislation is complicated enough to justify many weeks of deliberation, but that is the exception not the rule. |
| Show Committee | These are committees that are created for grandstanding purposes only. They often address legislation that appeal to a key voting block for the majority party. | The Michigan Senate Oversight Committee was formed in 2017 in the wake of the Center for Medical Progress videos implicating Planned Parenthood in the sale of baby parts for profit. The formation of the committee was greeted with much fanfare. I currently have a bill that would permanently defund Planned Parenthood in that committee that has yet to receive a hearing. My bill is not alone. In fact, the committee chair took no action on *any* legislation referred to this committee through the first eight months of its existence. |

| TACTIC | DESCRIPTION | COMMENTARY |
|---|---|---|
| Amend on the Floor | If pressed for time, it may be more expedient to amend a bill on the floor rather than ensure that a given bill is ready for implementation prior to being reported out of committee. | Agreements to amend a bill on the floor are not always associated with "swampy" intentions. It depends on the intentions of the bill sponsor, committee chair, and floor leader. Sometimes a bill can be reported to the floor with an agreement between the bill sponsor and a committee member to amend it on the floor that is later negated by actions taken by other parties. The net effect is that the bill is never amended as promised. |
| Government Ops | In many states, there is one committee where bills not supported by the leader of the respective chamber go to die kind of like the land of misfit toys in *Rudolph the Red Nose Reindeer*. | In the Michigan Senate, this committee is known as the Senate Government Operations Committee, which is chaired by the Senate majority leader. |
| The Naughty and Nice List | In much the same way as the chamber leader may have lists, committee chairs may create their own lists that could result in either the promotion or blockage of legislation from specific legislators. | In the wake of my vocal opposition to the medical marijuana expansion legislation, the committee chair that shepherded the passage of that legislation blocked legislation in his committee that I had introduced to close a loophole in state law and protect pilots from directed energy weapons such as lasers from being pointed at them during flight. As a result of his decision, the enactment of this commonsense law was delayed by a year until I was able to find a sponsor in the House that was not on his "Naughty List" to introduce and pass the same legislation. |

| TACTIC | DESCRIPTION | COMMENTARY |
|---|---|---|
| Horse Trading | Committee Chairs can be involved in "horse trading" activities in much the same way as chamber leaders are. That is why chairmanships of key committees can result in significant influence for certain legislators. | It pays to be assigned chairmanships for powerful committees. |
| "Special" Interests | Some committee chairs are designated as chairs of their respective committee to serve the best interests of special interests not the broader interests of the citizens of the state. These special interests often have significant influence over what bills are taken up in that committee and which bills are not through the committee chair. | Committees that align with the policy arena of generous special interest groups such as hospitals or energy companies are highly sought after by legislators seeking to have access to significant campaign contributions. |

## TACTIC

Leadership Cover

## DESCRIPTION

Leadership within the respective legislative chambers often make a big deal out of deferring to the judgment of the chair of a respective committee regarding the merit of a given bill or bill package. This tactic is often used to provide cover for the leader when the leader is seeking to bury or promote a given piece of legislation in a manner that diminishes any association between the legislation and the leader.

## COMMENTARY

This tactic gets exposed for what it really is when the opinion of the chair of a committee is in direct opposition to that of the chamber leader.

The old adage "power corrupts and absolute power corrupts absolutely" rings true even in the committee process.

### Floor Tactics

Floor tactics are a subset of the legislative process that deserve special attention as they can often have a significant influence upon the success or failure of legislation.

### Public Servant

The floor tactics for public servants are focused upon making sure that any legislation that did not pass through one of the committees upon which they serve receives sufficient scrutiny to discern whether or not it should be supported or opposed.

Public servants recognize the importance of principled deliberation in the legislative process. A common expression regarding the process for passing laws is that it is similar to sausage making in that you simply want it to taste good and don't care how it's made. Perhaps it is the engineer in me, but I believe that it is important to know how it's made, not just how good it tastes.

A sample list of tactics employed by public servants in this sausage making process is provided in Table 15. The bottom line is that public servants play by the rules.

### Swamp Servant

The floor tactics for swamp servants are focused upon finding ways to push legislation they support through the process regardless of its merit to the majority of citizens.

# TABLE 15: PUBLIC SERVANT FLOOR TACTICS

| TACTIC | DESCRIPTION | COMMENTARY |
|---|---|---|
| Roll Call Votes | When a vote is a roll call vote, the vote of each member of the chamber is recorded in the legislative journal for public access. | The advent of the internet has made tracking of legislator voting records easier than ever before. Voters can now view who voted yes or no on specific legislation or track the votes of their legislator on specific topics of interest to them. Because the bill explanations can sometimes be misleading, you should contact your legislator to inquire why they voted a certain way before jumping to too many conclusions. Remember the pitfalls of keyword legislation. |
| Debate | Members have the opportunity to debate the merit of a given piece of legislation on the floor of the chamber. This debate serves as an extension of committee discussion that includes all members of the chamber rather than simply the committee members. | The fact of the matter is that the fate of a given piece of legislation is decided behind closed doors in caucus deliberations well before it ever comes to the floor of each chamber for a vote. It is very rare that floor debates sway votes, but it does happen. |
| Floor Speeches | Members have the opportunity to make floor speeches that can be used to call attention to specific policy concerns and shape the public debate on a particular issue. | I make a point of ensuring that all of my public commentary is available for my constituents to review from my Senate website. |

| TACTIC | DESCRIPTION | COMMENTARY |
|---|---|---|
| Chamber Rules | Each chamber has a set of rules governing the conduct of business within each chamber. These rules deal with everything from the decorum expected by legislators to the rules for making motions on the floor. | One of the rules of the Senate proceedings is that the lieutenant governor can only cast the deciding vote on a bill if the floor vote results in a tie. During consideration of legislation that would expand Medicaid in Michigan, I withheld my vote to temporarily block passage, as my vote would have otherwise resulted in a tie. |
| Caucus Rules | Each party caucus within each chamber adopts another set of rules that governs the election of caucus leadership, expectations regarding procedural votes such as Immediate Effect and other rules as warranted by caucus members. | Almost three years into my second four-year term in the Michigan Senate, in an attempt to hurt my bid for governor, the Senate majority leader removed me from all of my committee assignments. The explanation provided to the media alleged that I violated some unspecified caucus rule. There was no violation of any written caucus rule, but the fact that most people are not even aware that there is a such thing as "caucus rules" provided convenient cover for what was in reality a petty abuse of authority on the part of the Senate majority leader. |

# TABLE 16: SWAMP SERVANT FLOOR TACTICS

| TACTIC | DESCRIPTION | COMMENTARY |
| --- | --- | --- |
| Voice Votes | Legislators avoid roll call votes that are recorded in the legislative journal by taking voice votes. Members motioning for Yeas and Nays and receiving commensurate support for such a motion typically can overrule voice votes. | Nikki Haley rose to prominence in the South Carolina legislature by challenging the good ole boy network in the state House to be more accountable for their votes. |
| Discharge from Committee | If there are insufficient votes in committee to report a bill out of committee that is important to leadership, leadership may motion to discharge a bill from committee. | According to Michigan Senate caucus rules, the motion to discharge a bill from committee is a procedural vote that is to be supported by all members whether they support the legislation or not. |
| Reconsider the Vote | While there are legitimate reasons to reconsider a vote that are consistent with the rationale for this motion to be included in the floor rules for a given chamber, it is important to highlight that it is sometimes used to buy time to twist arms. | Earlier, I noted that I used a procedural maneuver to temporarily block the expansion of Medicaid in Michigan. It was temporary because the Senate majority floor leader at the time made a motion to reconsider the vote. Three hours later, the proponents of the bill had "encouraged" a former no vote to flip his vote to yes, and the bill was passed. Because the tie was broken, I proceeded to vote no that time. |

## TACTIC

Vehicle Bills

## DESCRIPTION

Vehicle bills are bills which open up the same section of law as a newly proposed piece of legislation but have already passed out of one chamber thereby reducing the time it takes to pass the new legislation. Vehicle bills are typically used exclusively for contentious pieces of legislation that leadership prefers to "pop up" on the legislative agenda for consideration.

## COMMENTARY

At the end of a lame duck session in 2014, leaders in the Michigan legislature had a dilemma on their hands. Their ill-conceived push for a tax increase proposal was stalled and time was running out on the legislative session for that year. If they were to introduce a new bill, it would not have met the requirements of Article IV, Section 26 of the Michigan Constitution, which specified that bills needed to spend 5 days in each chamber before voting and there were less than 10 days left in the session.

They needed to find a vehicle bill that opened the same section of law, and ironically, they used a bill that I sponsored to promote civics education in our schools. Leadership proceeded to substitute my bill with the language of the Democrat's bill. The change in subject matter was a clear violation of Article IV Section 24 of the Michigan Constitution which precludes changes in the intent of the legislation between chambers. When I formally requested that the Attorney General issue an opinion that would nullify the subsequent law, he put his political finger to the wind and decided that the enforcement of the Constitution would not be to his political advantage.

| TACTIC | DESCRIPTION | COMMENTARY |
|---|---|---|
| Referendum Proofing | Many states have a constitutional provision that precludes citizen referendums on appropriations bills. In light of this, some legislators have taken to including appropriations in legislation that primarily concerns policy. | Article II Section 9 of the Michigan Constitution explicitly excludes appropriations bills from referendums. |
| Sleep Deprivation | There are a variety of techniques employed to break the will of legislators regarding particularly contentious bills that take advantage of basic human frailties such as the need for sleep. Decision-making faculties tend to diminish after prolonged deprivation from sleep. | The Michigan House of Representatives has kept representatives in sessions for days at a time resulting in some legislators sleeping under their desks as leadership twisted arms to cast a particular vote. |
| Show Votes | Show votes on the floor often take the form of amendments introduced by the opposition party primarily for campaigning purposes with full knowledge that it will not pass nor would the impacts of its passage likely be practical. | Democrats routinely introduce budget amendments that give more money to their favorite voter demographic during our budget deliberations. During my first term in the Senate, I calculated one year that their amendments would have added over $2 billion to the budget without any identification of revenue source or commensurate expense reductions. |

## TACTIC

Selective
Rule
Enforcement

## DESCRIPTION

The selective enforcement of chamber rules or caucus rules is often employed by leadership to penalize or reward legislators who oppose them or support them respectively.

## COMMENTARY

The reason rules and laws are written down is so that leaders are not supposed to be able to enforce them in an arbitrary manner. If the rules are hidden, however, it makes it much easier for leadership to abuse their authority.

In contrast to public servants, Swamp servants attempt to use the rules to keep any public servants which oppose them at bay while they move their preferred legislation through the system.

### *Budget Tactics*

Budgets are simply legislation with dollar signs. In this context, the passage of budgets involves many of the same tactics inherent with the passage of any bill. Since the power of the purse is one of the most significant ways that the legislature wields its authority, though, it is worth looking into several tactics unique to the spending of the people's money.

### *Public Servant*

The principle objective of all public servants involved in the appropriations process is to ensure that the hard-earned tax dollars of our citizens is put to effective use for the public good.

# TABLE 17: PUBLIC SERVANT BUDGET TACTICS

| TACTIC | DESCRIPTION | COMMENTARY |
|---|---|---|
| Departmental Budgets | In order to promote effective oversight of the expenditures of each department, the legislative budget process typically starts with a unique appropriations bill for each department. | My first act as budget chair of the state police and Department of Military and Veterans Affairs was to ask for a comprehensive list of services provided by each department correlated with the cost of such services. These services were categorized into core services (i.e., the reason for the department), support services (e.g., HR, IT, Accounting), and work projects (e.g., IT system deployment). Once this list was defined, we worked together on defining reasonable performance metrics for each service. We established a quarterly metrics review cycle to ensure that the departments were on target towards their objectives. This approach resulted in more accountability for tax dollars and dramatic performance improvements. |
| Supplementals | Supplemental appropriation bills can be made to adjust departmental budgets throughout the year in response to variations from forecast revenue projections. | Supplemental budget appropriations used in conjunction with the departmental oversight regimen that I instituted as budget chair provides an opportunity make adjustments to departmental budget based on performance. |

| TACTIC | DESCRIPTION | COMMENTARY |
|---|---|---|
| Points of Difference | Typically, there are variations between the department budgets passed out of each chamber. Negotiations between budget chairs to resolve these variations are supposed to be limited to points of differences. | Most times, these points of differences can be resolved between the House and Senate chairpersons. These resolutions typically feature good faith compromises and horse trading. |
| Rollup | Rolling up budget line items to larger budget line items effectively gives the executive branch more latitude as to how funds within a given department are expended unless there are boilerplate provisions that dictate additional oversight provisions. | As chair of the State Police and Department of Military and Veterans Affairs budgets, I rolled up the funding line items but unrolled the boilerplate items. In the boilerplate, I specified specific performance metrics requirements that we monitored on a quarterly basis. This approach provides departments with more flexibility to achieve their specified performance objectives. Typically, the chairs of the budget would only meet with department officials on an annual basis. |
| Unroll | Unrolling the resolution of budget line items effectively inserts additional legislative oversight into the budget process. | Unrolling a budget can be used a substitute for diligent oversight between budget deliberations. If the department is constrained by a detailed list of line item appropriations, they need to go to the legislature for approval of any reallocation of funds at a low level of budget detail. This approach provides departments with less flexibility on how best to achieve any performance objectives that may have been specified. |

## TABLE 18: SWAMP SERVANT BUDGET TACTICS

| TACTIC | DESCRIPTION | COMMENTARY |
|---|---|---|
| Omnibus | An omnibus budget is when multiple department budgets are rolled up into a single, large budget in an attempt to force an up or down vote on the entire budget rather than individual departments. | Omnibus budgets are often used to provide cover for members who may have issues with some provisions of a budget but are otherwise favorable to the majority of other provisions. |
| Everything is a Point of Difference | Committee deliberations on individual budget items can be circumvented by a procedural move that grants line item authority to leadership during final negotiations between the governor, Senate majority leader, and Speaker. This committee override is enabled when both chambers introduce appropriations bills for the same department. The bill from one of the chambers is then "zeroed out" effectively making everything in the bill a "point of difference" subject to direct manipulation by the governor, Senate majority leader, and Speaker. This tactic effectively nullifies the purpose of the committee process as it results in final conference reports that have been carved out by the governor, Senate majority leader, and Speaker, not the committee chairs. | The Senate majority leader used this tactic repeatedly during my first term in office to include funding line items for influential donors which I had explicitly removed from the budget during committee deliberations. |

## TACTIC

Bury It

## DESCRIPTION

Funding for certain projects or products can be buried in a budget by making a vague allusion to the item in the legislation. The broader the interpretation, the easier it is to bury it.

## COMMENTARY

It is incumbent upon the committee chair overseeing the pertinent budget to ensure adequate transparency of expenditures although sometimes these line items can be inserted by leadership without the awareness of committee chairs when everything in the budget is a "point of difference."

The budget oversight responsibilities of the legislature are some of the most important duties of an elected official. The government would theoretically run effectively without a single policy bill being passed during a legislative session. The same cannot be said if there were no appropriations bill passed.

### Swamp Servant

In contrast to the principle objective of public servants, swamp servants tend to use the budget process to reward themselves or their benefactors.

My focus is upon making sure that the distribution of limited tax dollars is fair, constitutional, and consistent with my campaign promises.

# 11

# WHAT HAPPENS
# WHEN ONE UPSETS THE "SWAMP"?

During the 2016 Presidential Campaign, I was sitting in bed after a long day reading Senator Ted Cruz's book, *A Time for Truth*. When I started reading the chapter called Mendacity, I stopped and called over to Angie, who was almost asleep, 'you've got to hear this.' I resumed reading the chapter aloud so that she could hear. We were both riveted as Ted gave us a peak behind the curtain of how policy decisions are really made in the US Senate. It was eerily similar to how they were made in the Michigan State Senate.

The book is filled with examples of what happened when Senator Cruz had the audacity to stay true to his principles as he challenged the "Swamp" in DC. My wife repeatedly blurted out, "that's you!" while I was reading. In fact, one of the Michigan Senate Democrats pejoratively had referred to me as "Michigan's Ted Cruz" in a fund-raising letter earlier that year. It was clearly a badge of honor.

This may come as a surprise to many of you, but the Swamp does not take kindly to elected officials who challenge its priorities. As circumstances have it, my priorities as a public servant are often at odds with those of Swamp servants. My priorities are as follows:

1. Best interests of our citizens at large
2. Fulfilling campaign promises
3. Party platform
4. Senate and House leadership

You may recall the Swamp priorities from earlier in the book. You may have noticed that my priorities are diametrically opposed to the priorities of the Swamp. This often makes the Capitol a "hostile work environment."

While it may not seem like it to the general public, I know that I am not alone within our caucus as an advocate of these priorities. What differs between the various members is the degree to which we will stand up for these priorities. No one wants to be at the center of conflict, especially conflict with those who control the movement of your legislation or access to donors needed for your next election. Each member performs a political calculation as to whether or not the likelihood of success in fighting the system is worth the risks.

My political calculus is rather straightforward. Does it honor my oath of office? In Michigan, that oath reads as follows:

> I do solemnly swear that I will support the Constitution of the United States and the constitution of this state, and that I will faithfully discharge the duties of the office of State Senator according to the best of my ability. So help me God.

Much like those who currently serve us or have served us in uniform, I take this oath very seriously. If a decision honors this oath of office, then, yes, I do it. If it doesn't, I don't. I did not choose politics as a career. I am not concerned about my next job. I fully trust that where God guides, He provides. I chose to serve, and not just serve. I committed to serve to the best of my ability.

My priorities put the people at the top because Article I, Section 1 of the Michigan Constitution reads, "All political power is inherent in the *people*. Government is instituted for their *equal* benefit, security and protection" (emphasis mine).

I would not be honoring my oath of office if I were to prioritize special interests over the best interests of the people at large. I know this may seem kind of strange in today's day and age. I get it. But it is the way we are supposed to approach public service.

There are repercussions, however, for elected officials who vocally oppose the Swamp and its priorities.

What happens when one violates these unwritten rules?

One of the repercussions is that you could be banned from caucus. Such was the case with State Representative Harvey Santana. Representative Santana is a Democrat who is known for working with Republicans on various issues important to the constituents in his district. What is wrong with that? Well, you see, the Democratic Caucus voted on what is meant by being a "team player." Representative Santana violated these "team player" rules when he sought the best interests of his constituents. He was literally escorted out of the House Democratic Caucus as a result.

I have toured Representative Santana's district with him. He knows his constituents. In fact, my tour reminded me of the *Seinfeld* episode that features Jerry walking the streets of New

York as a postman giving a warm hello to everyone as he walks by. While I do not always agree with Representative Santana's policy positions, I am confident that he believes that he is serving the best interests of his constituents.

Representative Santana had the last laugh. He was appointed the vice chairman of appropriations by the new Republican Speaker of the House. As a result, he became arguably the most powerful member of the House Democratic Caucus as all Democratic spending requests would need to go through him.

Penalties are not only enforced by Swamp Democrats, they are also inflicted by Swamp Republicans. In fact, I was the target of such enforcement. The enforcement was not quite as dramatic as being escorted out of the caucus, but it did get noticed by our friends in the media who understand how the system works.

In the wake of the 2014 election, Republicans retained control of the Michigan Senate with a 27-11 majority. Within days of the election, the Senate Republican Caucus held leadership elections. In these elections, the Senate majority floor leader, Senator Arlan Meekhof, was unanimously elected to the position of Senate Majority Leader. Senator Meekhof comes from arguably the most conservative Senate district in the State of Michigan. At that time, he had a reputation as a conservative legislator with a conservative rating somewhere between 80 and 89 percent according to the American Conservative Union. As arguably the most conservative legislator in the Senate, I thought this would bode well for the upcoming legislative session. It should be a relief, I thought, after serving under Senate Majority Leader Randy Richardville, whose voting record and policy preferences reflected the interests of his much less conservative district. I was certainly looking forward to the changing of the guard.

January 2015 signaled the start of a new legislature with the new Senate Majority Leader. January 2015 also featured new committee assignments including chairmanships. The release of such assignments is highly anticipated by members of the media, members of the lobbying establishment, and, of course, by elected officials. It is customary for the incoming Senate Majority Leader to discuss such assignments with members of his respective caucus before sharing with the media.

I didn't know it at the time, but my service in my first term had earned me the apparent disdain of influential members of the Swamp. In appreciation for my efforts, I was the only Republican Senator not to sit as chairman of any committee. While I was assigned to serve on several committees, (although I have since been removed from all committees in an attempt to silence my voice during my campaign for Governor) the incoming leader made sure I was seated in the junior Senator position on each of these committees (except for one on which I serve as vice chair) so as to not exert any undue influence on any committee vote. (Junior Senators vote last.)

I first learned of what was dubbed as a "committee snub" from the media. In fact, my first clue that something was amiss came by way of a tweet from a Lansing-based journalist.

"Incoming Senate Majority Leader @ArlanMeekhof just announced committee chairmanships for 2015. Second-term senator @pjcolbeck got nothing." December 22, 2014 from Chad Livengood of the *Detroit News*.

Before I jumped to any conclusions, I decided to text the incoming Senate Majority Leader for confirmation. I asked if it were true that I did not receive any committee chairmanships. He replied simply, "You didn't earn it."

A subsequent story by the *Detroit News* on January 2, 2015, summarized the issue as follows:

> Incoming Senate Majority Leader **Arlan Meekhof**, R-West Olive, announced committee chairmanships last week and all but one member of the 27-member Republican caucus got a chairman's gavel.
>
> Sen. **Patrick Colbeck**, R-Canton, is returning for a second term and has chaired the state police and military affairs department subcommittee of the Appropriations Committee for the past four years. Meekhof instead assigned second-term Sen. **Mike Nofs**, R-Battle Creek, to chair that subcommittee next year.
>
> It's unusual for a second-term majority party senator *not* to chair a committee. Six incoming freshman senators will be chairing committees next year, according to Meekhof's assignment list, but Colbeck will not.
>
> Meekhof spokeswoman **Amber McCann** said the new leader assigned chairmanships based on each individual senator's "experience, interest and expertise."
>
> "Sen. Colbeck has shown a particular interest in working in his district with constituents and also participating in conferences and seminars," McCann told Insider. "Sen. Meekhof just tried to be considerate of Colbeck's schedule and his passion."
>
> Colbeck did not return a message seeking comment."

Happy New Year!

I have come around to forgiving Senator Meekhof for his actions. I continue to struggle with trusting him, but I do forgive him.

To this day, I do not know what truly motivated him to take the actions that he did. At that point in my service, I had never had a cross word with him. I do not know if he had issues with me personally or whether or not he was acting on behalf of others who had influence over him.

Mind you, I had never discussed my "particular interests" with the incoming Senator Majority Leader, although I appreciate his apparent recognition of the importance that I place upon my constituents. In light of this it is easy to see, however, how the Swamp could see it as a conflict. My priorities are the best interests of my constituents not special interests. As a point of fact, though, I don't view prioritizing the best interests of my constituents as something that conflicts with the duties of serving as the chairman of a committee. It certainly did not impair in the least my effectiveness as chairman of the Department of Military and Veterans Affairs (DMVA) and Michigan State Police (MSP) budgets in my first term. In fact, my work in that capacity is highly respected by those interested in improving the transparency and effectiveness of these budget areas. We created a new structure that provided more transparency of budget line items and began tracking the progress immediately. During the four years in which I served as the Senate chair for these budgets, the improvements were dramatic.

The Michigan Department of Military and Veterans Affairs has two primary functions: 1) advise veterans of the benefits for which they are eligible, and 2) provide the Federal Veterans Affairs Agency with the benefit claims information needed to process veteran claims effectively. Function 1 is not as easy as it might seem. There are literally dozens of state and federal programs for which a veteran or active duty serviceman or servicewoman might be eligible. There was little or no standardization of this information in the department. And it was difficult to know who was a veteran in our state. We had a rough idea that 680,000 veterans called Michigan home, but we did not have a contact list so that we could reach them. In order to address this issue, the adjutant general, Greg Vadnais, his assistant, Michael Stone, and metrics guru Ann Zerbe launched a "No wrong door" policy and created the Michigan Veterans Affairs Agency that would track all of the state's veterans. Our next challenge was to provide the VA with the claims information. Michigan was ranked fifty-third out of fifty-three states and territories in getting veterans the benefits they earned. Part of the problem was that only 4 percent of the claims submitted on behalf of our veterans in the state were what is called "fully developed." That means that the VA did not have sufficient information to process the claim 96 percent of the time! The new Michigan Veterans Affairs Agency began tracking the fully developed claims in its quarterly review. The Agency went on to establish a Service Level Agreement with our Veteran Service Organizations. Prior to the end of my tenure as chair of the DMVA budget, we improved our fully developed claims rate from 4 percent to over 52 percent. This 52 percent rate was good enough to elevate Michigan from one of the worst states in the nation to second place. In practical terms, most Michigan veterans will now receive their benefits as fast as the Federal VA system can process their claims. Our team's achievements must not have exemplified the "experience, interest, and expertise" that Senator Meekhof was looking for.

The Michigan State Police budget was a bit more complicated. When I started my service as Senate Chairman of the State Police budget, Michigan had the dubious distinction of having four of our cities on the FBI's Top 10 Most Dangerous Cities list. This was due in part to the loss of law enforcement resources at all levels during the Lost Decade, during which time trooper strength declined from 1,344 in 2000 to 975 in 2011. We also had significant backlogs in crime lab case management. The average turnaround time to local law enforcement and prosecutors for specialized crime lab services was sixty-six days. When the city of Detroit filed for bankruptcy and had to close the crime lab, they discovered that there were almost ten thousand rape kits that had not been analyzed. That translates to ten thousand incidents of rape for which there would be no justice. In short, it was not a very satisfactory state of affairs.

The good news was that I found many kindred spirits in the State Police. Under the exceptional leadership of Colonel Kristie Etue, Shawn Sible, and Sherri Irwin, I found the State Police to be a very professional and metrics-driven organization. We worked well together and converted what had been a fairly opaque budget into a very transparent one. With this new budget framework, we met with an extremely professional cadre of state police officials and local law enforcement professionals to systematically prioritize the services and resources required. Our trooper strength grew to 1,184. We didn't just grow in numbers; we grew in reach. In order to stretch these limited resources further, we closed posts and leveraged in-vehicle technology to keep troopers on the road. This improved flexibility allowed us to deploy resources where they were most needed. We launched a Secure Cities initiative that augmented existing law enforcement with temporary state and county resources. At the beginning of 2016, only one city remained on the FBI's Top 10 list of most violent cities in America.[1] We added ten lab technicians and upgraded equipment resulting in a reduction in average turnaround time to fifty days. By the end of my tenure, all of the Detroit rape kits had been analyzed, which resulted in a new problem outside of my budget area: a prosecution backlog. Once again, it appears that this was not the sort of leadership Senator Meekhof was looking for.

The quarterly review process that I started for both the DMVA and MSP budgets continues to keep us on track towards our joint objectives to this day. There is a significant body of evidence to suggest that budget transparency and service delivery were drastically improved during my tenure as chair of these budgets.

In this light, I was very curious about why the incoming Senate Majority Leader believed that I "did not earn it." Before I commented publicly on the Senate Majority Leader's decision and subsequent statement, though, I felt it best to have a face-to-face meeting with him to find out what drove his decision.

He agreed to the meeting. During the meeting, I asked him what he meant by saying that I did not "earn" a chairmanship. He proceeded to give me the following four reasons in order why he believed that I did not "earn" a chairmanship:

1.  My vocal opposition to Medicaid Expansion
2.  My vocal opposition to Common Core
3.  I had underperformed in my recent election for State Senate
4.  A dispersion against my fellow colleagues in the Senate that I would prefer not to share

Regarding the first assertion, I had indeed been very vocal in my opposition to Medicaid Expansion. In fact, I went well beyond just saying No. I even offered an alternative solution (SB 459 and 460 of 2013) based upon Direct Primary Care Services that would improve care for Medicaid enrollees while saving taxpayers billions of dollars. These bills were never given serious consideration by leadership. As I explained earlier, the euphemistically called Healthy Michigan (aka Medicaid Expansion, aka Section 2001 of HR 3590, aka Obamacare) bill was the one for which I withheld my vote to prevent then-Lt. Gov. Brian Calley an opportunity to break the tie and vote in favor of the legislation. If you remember, Senator Meekhof bought time and twisted the arm of another Senator to get his twenty votes. This bill was bad policy, clearly opposed in our Republican platform, opposed by the majority of my Republican colleagues, opposed by *all* of the Republican US Senators called to vote on Obamacare, and is currently in an automatic repeal death spiral due to shortfalls on savings projections. And according to Senator Meekhof, my opposition to this bill was viewed as a disloyal act. His view towards Medicaid Expansion clearly does not represent the views of the majority of Republicans.

Regarding the second assertion, I had indeed been very vocal in my opposition to Common Core Standards. As a member of the Senate Education Policy Committee, I had heard the arguments on both sides. I repeatedly asked for proof that the standards would actually improve the performance of our students. The so-called proof came two years after the standards had been adopted in Michigan in the form of a white paper titled "Curricular Coherence and the Common Core State Standards for Mathematics" by Professors Schmidt and Houang of Michigan State University. The paper attempted to convey a positive correlation between standards that aligned with Common Core and performance on the nationwide NAEP (National Assessment of Educational Progress) assessment. A rudimentary statistical analysis, however, revealed no such correlation. In fact, one could make the case that a negative correlation would have just as much statistical validity. Even the paper's authors noted, "Unfortunately determining the relationship between these new standards and achievement will take several years at the very least."[2] So yes, I was opposed to a group of elitist educrats who thought it was reasonable to experiment with an entire generation of our kids while enriching their coffers through the sales of new textbooks, new assessments, new lesson plans, and new professional development seminars. In the final analysis, I was joined in my opposition to Common Core by a National Republican Committee resolution, a Michigan State Republican Committee resolution, and numerous Republican Congressional District Republican Committees. Despite such support from the leadership of the Republican Party, my opposition to Common Core was viewed as a disloyal act by the incoming Republican Senate Majority Leader.

Regarding the third assertion, I had indeed underperformed in my 2014 reelection bid. The district was supposed to be a 55 percent Republican district yet I only received 52 percent of the general election vote. In my defense, I believe there were good reasons for these results. Due to my leadership role in the passage of Right to Work in Michigan and principled, conservative stands on many other issues, I was one of only two Michigan Republicans who were targeted by the National Democratic Party in our state's election cycle. Furthermore, I have it on good authority that individuals influential in the allocation of contributions to candidates encouraged Republican donors to divert contributions from my contested campaign to the Senate Republican Campaign Committee (SRCC) instead. In that way, the SRCC could keep me on a short leash. If I played ball, I would receive their full support. If not, I would not receive their full support. It was as simple as that.

During the lead-up to the election, I ignored the leash. I was a vocal opponent to a proposed tax hike to raise money for road repair. It is worth noting that I was subsequently supported in this opposition by 81 percent of the voters in Michigan. As before, I went beyond opposing the system's solution to offering a solution of my own that did not require a tax increase. My solution focused on building higher quality roads. I am confident that if it weren't for the fact that my seat was needed in order to ensure a twenty-six-seat supermajority at the time, I would not have received any significant support from the SRCC. In the final analysis, I did not play ball, and it was seen as grounds for me riding the Senate equivalent to the bench.

Concerning Senator Meekhof's fourth and final assertion regarding my colleagues, suffice it to say that I am upset by his views. Enough said.

If the Swamp were to prioritize the best interests of the general public or even the best interests of the fellow members of the party, the Senate Majority Leader never would have gotten away with the reasons cited previously to keep me out of leadership positions that would influence key policy decisions on behalf of our citizens. In such a system, leadership would seek to place the most experienced, most knowledgeable, and most dedicated personnel in the position best situated to serve the public good.

That's not what happened. There are repercussions for pushing back on the Swamp's priorities.

In the wake of my meeting with Senator Meekhof, my response was the following statement on the Senate floor:

"Why are you here?

Why did you subject yourselves, your family, and your friends to the lies, character assassinations, and hardships of all sorts that are all too often associated with running for elected office?

Are you here because you like being called Senator?

Do you like the power and prestige that may go along with the title?

Perhaps your motives are more noble.

Perhaps you have seen bad government in action and want to make sure that bad policies are replaced with good policies.

Perhaps members of your community lobbied you to be their voice in Lansing because they respect you.

Perhaps you simply want to serve others.

Many of you may have started out your public service with the noblest of intentions. Is that still what drives you today?

Politicians consistently poll in the single digits when citizens are asked which professions they trust. This lack of trust translates into a lack of trust in our political system, a political system that has brought our nation unparalleled prosperity, a precious spirit of generosity and status as a beacon of hope for the rest of the world.

*We need to restore trust in our political system.*

While it is no small task, this is the mission that motivates me to serve. We need to move beyond politics as usual and foster a political environment that restores the public's trust in our system of government.

Too often in Lansing, we find ourselves caught up in a cesspool of playground politics filled with false narratives, whisper campaigns, and attempts to elevate oneself by demeaning another.-

**We are better than this.**

*Together*, we can convert Lansing into an environment that promotes nobler virtues worthy of our proud American heritage, worthy of today's electorate, worthy of our posterity.
Virtues such as honesty and integrity.

Virtues such as freedom.

Virtues such as the promotion of the idea that our citizens deserve the BEST solutions to the problems that we face not simply A solution that benefits only an influential subset of our citizens.

It was painful whenever I encountered people on the campaign trail who had given up on our system of government, who had given up on the promise of a government they could trust, who had given up on the idea that any politician would put the best interests of their constituents above their own self-interests, who had given up on the idea that an elected official would legislate in a manner consistent with their campaign promises.

At risk is the very concept of living under a government that is

**of** the people,

**for** the people and

**by** the people.

Each of us reaffirmed the following oath last week.

"I do solemnly swear that I will support the Constitution of the United States and the constitution of this state, and that I will faithfully discharge the duties of the office of State Senator according to the best of my ability. So help me God"

Please note that we did not swear an oath to serve our own best interests.

We did not swear an oath to serve our favorite lobbying group.

We did not swear an oath to a specific individual.

We took an oath under God with our hands on the Bible to serve the best interests of "We the People."
This same Bible tells us that "No servant can **serve two masters.** Either you will hate the one, and love the other, or you will be devoted to the one and despise the other." (Luke 16:13).

I am asking each of us including myself to reflect upon a simple question.

Whom are you serving?

Are you serving the best interests of **ALL** of the Citizens of this state? If not, **why** not?

Are you afraid?

Are you afraid to speak up for what you know in your heart is right?

Are you afraid of being misrepresented and ridiculed in the media?

Are you simply afraid that you may not be up to the task?

I implore each of you. *Do not be afraid.*

For God did not give us a spirit of timidity or fear, but one of power, **of love** and of self-control.

I believe *that* is how we are called to serve.

In today's political environment, so often driven by self-interest, there doesn't seem to be any room for the pursuit of ideals bigger than oneself.

**We can change that.**

*Together*, we can provide our citizens with the quality of public service that *truly* earns the salutation of "Honorable."

It all starts with each of us answering a simple question with complete honesty:

Whom do you serve?"

It really is as simple as that. Whom do you serve? It is a question that every elected official should ask himself or herself on a regular basis. This question is more important now than ever.

Is it any wonder why the vast majority of our elected representatives simply keeps their heads down and follows the herd? Is it any wonder why Donald Trump was so successful with his "Drain the Swamp" messaging in the 2016 presidential election? Our citizens are now paying much better attention to whose priorities are being served, and they are rightly feeling left out.

A common cry from Americans all over the nation is "why don't our elected officials listen?" It is clear from my tenure in the Michigan Senate that there is nothing wrong with their hearing. They are listening. The problem is to whom they are listening. They are listening to the people who have provided them the financial backing needed to obtain their current position not the people who provided them with their vote. This needs to change. Respect for our system of government is at stake.

# PART 3

# DRAINING THE SWAMP

# 12

# IMPORTANT GOVERNANCE PRINCIPLES

In 1776, George Mason drafted a Declaration of Rights for Virginia that conveyed individual rights over the right of the government. In 1787, George Mason refused to sign the newly drafted Constitution until the Convention members agreed to add to it the Bill of Rights, which was similar to his Declaration of Rights. He said that "no free government, or the blessings of liberty can be preserved to any people, but by frequent recurrence to fundamental principles."

I do not believe that I am alone in my observation that our government has veered away from the principles that have made our nation truly exceptional. If there is one key takeaway from our last presidential election, it is that the American people are tired of what has become "politics as usual." Republicans, Independents, and Democrats are all looking for a better future. It is increasingly evident that there is no room in this future for politics as usual.

People have had it with smarmy politicians who kiss babies, poor coffee while sharing trite pleasantries, smile and cry on cue, and talk a lot but do very little. People are tired of elected officials who avoid taking a stand on issues that some might see as politically incorrect, ignore the Constitution, spend our tax money irresponsibly, and break their campaign promises shortly after they are sworn into office.

I, too, have had it with politics as usual. My mission is not to add more legislative volumes to law libraries around our state. It is not to build up the largest campaign war chest. It is not to enrich my own personal fortune. It is not to make sure that I have a cushy job after I am termed out of office.

My mission is to change our political environment.

It is my mission to show that principled service is still possible.

It is my mission to demonstrate that principled service is not only possible, but it is the best way to reach agreement on solutions that serve the best interests of the majority of our citizens.

It has been over seven years now since I first made the commitment to serve in public office, and my record is available for all to see. As I reflect upon this service, I believe that I have consistently adhered to these principles, but ultimately it is the opinions of my constituents that matter.

As I mentioned previously, the principles outlined in my Vote Compass were an attempt to align my principles with the principles of others with whom I would be serving. Over the course of the past seven years, I have developed the following set of seven corollaries to these principles. These corollaries provide additional clarity as to what guides my approach to problem solving on behalf of the best interests of our citizens.

### Government Works for the People

The government works for the people not the other way around. The United States Constitution starts with the words "We the people." Our Constitution is a contract or social compact between the people of our great nation and those whom they have elected to represent them. True power resides in the people. In fact, Article I Section I of the Michigan Constitution starts with the words "All political power is inherent in the people."

It is important for our elected officials to remember for whom they work. In Michigan, a battle over how best to fix our crumbling roads served as a startling example of how some legislators have forgotten for whom they work.

Michigan roads and bridges were in relatively poor condition across the state. The annual transportation budget for Michigan's 120,000 miles of roads and 10,711 bridges was about $3.3 billion. The Michigan Department of Transportation (MDOT) estimated that another $1.2 billion was needed to keep the transportation system from degrading further yielding a total budget requirement of $4.5 billion.

Against this backdrop, a 2014 Reason Foundation study reported that Michigan spent 53 percent more per mile while we were ranked forty-third in quality. We were not getting the value for our tax dollar. Our constituents knew this first-hand as they drove every day across our state on roads that fell apart within five years of building them. Consequently, I relentlessly pushed for higher quality road construction as a solution rather than to simply keep wasting money on more lousy roads.

That's not what happened. During the 2014 Lame Duck session, my colleagues were pressured into voting for a $2 billion tax increase. (Taxpayer money was even used to promote tax increases.) Sadly, only $400 million would have ended up going to roads initially. Fortunately, the proposal went down in flames when presented as a referendum to the people with 81 percent of voters saying No.

So how did the legislature respond? Within two months of the rejection of Proposal 1, Senate leadership responded with a proposal to increase the gas tax and vehicle registration fees by $600 million—this time without a vote of the people.

Why would they do that? In response to the proposal, I challenged my colleagues to a debate. All of them. None of the leaders of the tax increase proposal took me up on the challenge, although there was a Democratic Senator who did so in an ill-fated attempt to score political points.

In the end, the $600 million tax increase was passed after much arm-twisting and issue fatigue. Shortly after passage, $400 million from the general fund that had been allocated to fix our roads was transferred to other administration "priorities." The "roads crisis" was a red herring. Some in government needed a crisis to justify increasing taxes so that they could fill potholes in failed programs like Medicaid Expansion.

### Government Solutions Should Be for All Citizens

Government solutions need to prioritize the best interests of all citizens not simply a select few with access to power brokers. Article I Section I of the Michigan Constitution states "government is instituted for their *equal benefit*, security and protection."

One of the questions on my Vote Compass is "Will it be applied equally to *all* citizens?" Most of the bills which have earned my no vote have violated this simple principle.

One of the first examples of a bill that singled out a specific group of people that came to the Senate floor for a vote was SB 265 of 2011. The bill amended the Michigan Vehicle Code to create an exception to seasonal weight restrictions for vehicles transporting heating fuel. These weight restrictions were put in place during the spring thaw to protect roads from excessive deterioration. Why should heating fuel trucks be the only ones exempt from these weight restrictions? What about gasoline or milk trucks? Their lobbyists did not ask for the bill. The heating fuel lobbyists did. In general, the narrower the scope of a bill, the less likely it is to have opposition, and such was the case for this bill as it passed the Senate by a 25-12 vote. I was one of the no votes.

Truth be told, I have voted for bills with provisions that singled out specific groups of people. In such cases, I evaluate whether or not the bill moves towards the fulfillment of this principle or away from this principle. I refer to bills that move in the right direction as "needle movers." These bills often earn my support. Bills that create a precedent for special treatment of one group of people will typically earn my opposition.

This principle raises another important point. We need to dilute concentrations of power in both the state and federal government. Local governments know best what the priorities of their communities are. They know which roads need to get fixed. They know what schools provide the best learning environments. They know which streets need to get patrolled. Are there abuses of power in local government? Yes, but that does not mean that we should concentrate power in state and federal government officials. State and federal governments have an important oversight role to guard against abuses in local governments, but we need to stop the disturbing trend of absorbing more and more resources to grow state and federal government and thus leaving fewer and fewer resources for local governments.

### *Government Needs to Be Transparent*

The people should have more information about the government than the government has about the people. If you surf the web, own a smartphone, pay income taxes, attend school, use health insurance, use a credit card, or have a smart meter installed at your home, you are sharing information about your life with strangers.

Many engineers design and build what are called "control systems." Examples of control systems are the thermostat on your home, an airplane autopilot, or the computer programs and mechanical equipment that I used to regulate the atmosphere aboard the International Space Station. Control systems feature sensors, effectors, and a controller. Sensors, such as temperature or pressure sensors, feed the controller(s) with data. Using complex algorithms the controller(s) then manage the state of one or more variables collected by the sensors. Based on the logic in these algorithms and data provided by the sensors, the controllers send signals to effectors within the control system such as a furnace or airplane control surface. The more data one has, the more precise the ability of the control engineer to manage the desired system.

Just how much information that I am sharing on a daily basis really hit home with me about a year ago. I was an early adopter of smartphone technology. They certainly can make life so much easier. Case in point is getting directions. I still remember how my wife used to prompt me to stop at a gas station to ask for directions whenever we were uncertain about where we were headed. With the advent of the Internet, we would look up directions and then print them out to bring along with us on our trip. Now, we simply click on our destination captured in my online calendar and receive turn-by-turn directions based upon our GPS location. It turns out that all of this information is stored. I only needed to go to Location History on my Google Account to find out where I was all the way back to 2009. I can find out which restaurant I was at and how long I was there. I can track where we went on vacation. Useful information if I ever wanted to take a trip down memory lane.

More important is how others use this information. Invariably, information is used to influence behavior. In other words, information is about control. The more information one has about another individual or group of individuals, the more one can influence their behavior.

Marketing organizations have hit the jackpot with the advent of the Internet. Browsing the web reveals breadcrumbs called cookies that share information on where you've been on the web. Online retailers monitor your order history and your search history. Energy utilities use smart meter technology to monitor what appliances are used when in your home.

Government is no exception. It starts with income tax filings. The government knows how much money you make, the size of your home, which charities you support, and where you work. It may comfort you to know that the government tracks criminal records although its ability to do so effectively across all facets of the criminal justice system leaves much to be desired. Handoffs between the court system, prison system, jail system, parole system, and probation system leave much to be desired. It may surprise you to know, though, how much the government knows about your children. Under the auspices of the Common Core Standards Initiative, the federal government has promoted a Longitudinal Data System that collects over four hundred data items on your child that goes well beyond their performance on standardized tests. The Soviet Union used to ask kids questions about their parents. Did they go to church? Do they own a gun? We are now capturing the same sort of information right here in the United States.

A real gold mine for government control advocates has been health care. As one of the few individuals who have actually read HR 3590, it is clear that the federal health care policy known as Obamacare is all about control not care. It puts the pre-Obamacare administrative state on steroids with the addition of 159 new federal organizations that come between a doctor and patient. These organizations feed off of information. This information is captured via electronic medical record (EMR) systems that Doctors use to "code" patient conditions so that they may receive the proper insurance payments. The latest CPT (current procedural terminology) coding standard required by the Centers for Medicare and Medicaid Services is ICD-10, which is the latest revision of the International Statistical Classification of Diseases and Related Health Problems (ICD). The ICD is a medical classification list by the World Health Organization (WHO) that contains codes for diseases, abnormal findings, complaints, social circumstances, and external causes of injury or diseases. It goes well beyond medical conditions to better understand how those conditions were caused. In other words, this standard supports the creation of a behavioral profile on each patient.

Thankfully, I have made some progress towards providing citizens with information about their government. The budgets that I prepared for the state police and Department of Military and Veterans Affairs were the first accomplishments towards this end. Another example is the transparency legislation that I passed in 2012 that requires the posting of how much we spend on government services by spending category for each agency in state government. You can find this information at www.tenmillionaccountants.com.

This book is a prime example of government transparency. Readers of this book will better understand how government really works so that citizens can rest some measure of control back from the government. Simply put, citizens should have more information about the government than the government has about the citizens.

Information is about control. If someone else has more information about you than you have about them, you are vulnerable to being influenced by them. In today's digital age, it is more important than ever that we the people have more information about the government than the government has about us. It is the only way to maintain the proper balance of power in the relationship between the government and the governed.

### Government officials Need to Play Their Position

The Constitution is very clear. The legislative branch makes laws. The executive branch executes laws. The judicial branch issues opinions on court cases.

If the Constitution says, "*all* legislative powers herein granted shall be vested in a Congress," why does Congress sit on its hands when people say that Supreme Court decisions are the "law of the land"? Why do we allow Presidents to unilaterally change the provisions of a law as President Obama did multiple times with his signature legislation Obamacare? Why is Congress allowed to color outside the lines of its enumerated powers defined in Article I Section 8 of the Constitution?

We all should be asking ourselves these questions. This is a lesson that I learned very early during my service as state senator.

I had been a management consultant for eleven years prior to my election, so, naturally, my first project was to restructure the delivery of government services. Within the first two weeks of winning my first election, I set about developing a revised organization structure for state government. I referred to this new organization as Service-Oriented Government. It would refocus each agency on their core mission and centralize support services such as HR, IT, and accounting. Not only would it make more efficient use of taxpayer resources, it would also improve the effectiveness of the core services of each agency. It was quite an elegant approach to state government, if I do say so myself.

The effort culminated in a presentation to one of my more seasoned colleagues. At the conclusion of the presentation, he burst my bubble by saying, "You are a state senator not the governor."

He was right. I was not playing my position.

I was able to legitimately introduce elements of this service-oriented approach to governance in subsequent years within the confines of my role as a state senator. I introduced and passed transparency legislation that organizes government expenditures in a manner that eases the transition to a service-oriented governance structure. Plus, as the former chair of the budgets for the Michigan State Police and Department of Military and Veterans Affairs, I was able to restructure the budget for these agencies to reflect a service-oriented governance approach.

The bottom line is that we cannot afford to let our government operations devolve into anarchy like a peewee hockey game where goalies sometimes like to get into the action and score goals on the other side of the rink. We are the longest lasting government under a single Constitution. We need to honor this achievement and pay attention to the bounds our Constitution places upon the operation of our government.

### Know Your Past to Change Your Future

It is vital to understand what you are changing *from* before you change *to* something else. As you may have noticed in my process flows above, I have a penchant for understanding how things work. In fact, I have found it very useful to understand fully how something currently works before proposing to change it to something else.

I first learned the importance of this approach to making changes as an engineer working on the International Space Station. As a young design engineer, I had proposed a change to the oxygen-nitrogen distribution system for the station that would reduce the weight of the space station by thousands of pounds and lower the cost of the program by millions of dollars. In order to implement the change, I needed to prepare and submit a change request, which is very similar to a bill request in the legislature. Boeing had a very systematic change evaluation process that involved two phases. The first phase was an engineering phase where change advocates made their case to a panel of experienced engineers called the Brown Room. The second phase was where the financial implications of the change were addressed. This phase featured a panel of experienced managers called the Green Room. It was a very responsible way to address changes on the most complex spacecraft ever developed.

The process turned out to be a great way for me to get a better picture of the overall space station design. It also provided me with excellent insights into the business implications of engineering design decisions. What struck me was how many different space station systems were impacted by my proposed design change. What also struck me was how disciplined the change process needed to be to effectively address such impacts. The change form included check boxes for each system needed for station operations, including ground support systems.

In the legislature, a bill represents a change request to our state laws. Bills reflect a desire to change the state of laws, departmental operations, expenditures, law enforcement standards, law enforcement training, and judicial penalty matrices. When I began serving in the Senate, I was struck by how little congressmen typically know about the current state of affairs before proposing changes to the system. The full impact of proposed legislation is rarely understood before being voted on.

To be fair, we do have House and Senate fiscal agencies that are tasked with the difficult chore of assessing the impact of proposed legislation. Michigan's full-time legislature pumps out almost four thousand pieces of legislation each legislative session. The analysis of this legislation falls upon the shoulders of a couple dozen analysts. Due to the volume of bills, analysis is typically postponed until a bill moves in committee. These agencies sometimes are given only twenty-four hours to assess what may be a fairly complex piece of legislation.

Legislators should ultimately bear the responsibility to understand the current system before proposing changes to it. This has been my modus operandi throughout my legislative tenure.

A prime example of this approach to public service was when I investigated our state procurement process in response to claims of excessive award challenges and failure to meet statutory obligations for veteran preferences. My first step was to map out the current procurement process in much the same way that I have done in the evaluation of government processes earlier in this book. I went on to analyze how we might mitigate challenges to contract awards via enhanced transparency. I also investigated how we might better achieve the objective of honoring the career sacrifices of our veterans on our behalf by incentivizing companies to hire more veterans. Once the analysis was complete, I introduced legislation that would reasonably achieve these objectives and prepared a presentation that would walk committee members through the rationale for the legislation.

Most legislators do not go through these steps. The process is much simpler for them. Step 1: receive a bill from a lobbyist. Step 2: introduce the bill from the lobbyist. Step 3: lobbyist lobbies other legislators for support. Note that lobbyists are not typically interested in legislators understanding the true current state of affairs before soliciting a vote on legislation.

Inherent in the system is the need for trust. The fiscal agencies have a couple dozen employees to analyze almost four thousand bills per year. Senators or representatives typically have the budget for a single paid staff member to analyze each bill on which they will vote. While I am pretty good about reading proposed legislation before voting, reading does not always translate to a solid understanding of the impact of the legislation before being compelled to vote on it. Sometimes, legislators only have minutes to read legislation before being asked to vote on it. These votes are often cast completely on the basis of trust in the impact assessment provided by the fiscal agency, bill sponsor, or legislative aid.

With these observations in mind, one can see why it is often necessary for legislators to take direct responsibility for analyzing legislation introduced by other members. That is exactly what I do on significant pieces of legislation. One of the most significant pieces of legislation I had to review was a proposal for Michigan to adopt the Obamacare state-based health exchanges. One of my Republican colleagues introduced this legislation even though it flew in the face of our Republican Platform. Clearly, trust was not going to cut it with this legislation. It didn't add up. I found it hard to believe that one of my Republican colleagues would be proposing this legislation, so I did some digging on my own. The legislation was billed as "giving Michigan control over our healthcare system." What I found was that it only gave the appearance of control. Like the Affordable Care Act, this bill also granted control of all major policy decisions to the secretary of the Department of Health and Human Services. States who adopted the so-called "state-based exchanges would simply be performing the legislative equivalent of painting Tom Sawyer's fence for him so to speak. My analysis was too late to move enough senators to stop this legislation in the Senate, but it helped to eventually defeat it in the House.

One of the most difficult parts of the job of legislator is to gain a true understanding of the impact of proposed legislation prior to voting on it. There are quite a few salesmen in state capitols across the nation who are exceedingly good at telling legislators what they want to hear. We need more legislators willing to go the extra mile and pursue the truth.

### Tax Increases Should Be the Last Option

Sir Winston Churchill once sagely opined during budget discussions, "Gentleman, we have run out of money. It is now time to think."

All too often, tax increases are the only solutions legislators think about. A clear example of the "tax first" mindset often on display by government officials was our previously mentioned roads debate.

Just to be clear. Taxes are not bad. Excessive taxation is bad. How do you determine if taxation is excessive or not? Define the social problem that is to be solved by the tax. If a majority of citizens agree that it is a serious problem, solutions to that problem should be identified by our elected representatives. If there are solutions to these problems that do not require tax or fee increases, they should be pursued before all others. If there are solutions that do not require a tax increase and yet legislatures vote to increase taxes or fees instead, the taxation would be excessive.

I still recall my orientation session shortly after being elected. I was treated to a non-partisan symposium on the need to raise taxes as the de facto solution for all of our budgetary ailments. It didn't take long for this issue to surface during my service in the Michigan Senate. Governor Snyder had proposed what was referred to as the Senior Pension Tax. The governor sought to raise $300 million in the form of a tax on fixed-income residents of our state.

Instead of supporting the tax, I identified $747 million in unnecessary expenses that could be cut as an alternative. The expense reduction options were not supported and the tax went on to barely pass in the Senate, where I voted No.

Michigan's escalating Medicaid budget represents another persistent budget area constantly seeking additional revenue, especially in the wake of the decision to expand Medicaid in our state. The default solution continues to be tax increases. In fact, they created a new tax on all health care claims called the Health Insurance Claims Assessment (HICA). HICA revenue is supposed to be used to help pay for the state's portion of Medicaid. As Medicaid expenses soar, the pressure to keep increasing HICA rates will continue to soar as well. I have persistently proposed alternatives to HICA rate increases. I am happy to report that my Direct Primary Care Services Medicaid Pilot provides a pathway to save taxpayers over $3.6 billion by improving preventive care. Patience is a virtue, but persistence to the point of success is a blessing.[1]

Bottom line, before I ask our hardworking taxpayers to fork out another dime in taxes, we need to take a hard look at *all* of our options. We should prioritize those options in a manner that recognizes that many of our citizens are already struggling to make ends meet. Whenever the legislature fails to seek alternatives to tax increases, all that they do is force our families to find more ways to pinch pennies.

### Promote First-Party Transactions

A first-party transaction is when you purchase a service for your personal benefit with your personal funds. They are the best way to control costs and promote quality because both parties are directly involved in the purchase decisions. This principle applies to pretty much any purchase decision.

I first heard of this expression when listening to a talk by former Congressman Bob McEwen (R-OH) at a ProFamily

Legislators Conference hosted by WallBuilders.[2] During his talk, he highlighted the differences between first-party, second-party, and third-party transactions.

A first-party transaction is when you purchase a service for your personal benefit with your personal funds. Cost and quality are concerns

A second-party transaction is when you purchase a service for someone else using your funds (e.g., a birthday gift). Cost generally is the primary driver when determining such a purchase.

A third-party transaction is when you purchase a service for someone else using someone else's funds. Neither quality nor cost are a principle concern in your purchase decision.

Almost all government transactions are third-party transactions.

Basically, the more we ensure that government policies promote first-party transactions, the more we promote higher quality services that cost less.

# 13

# BOLD-COLORED SOLUTIONS

In his 1975 CPAC Speech, President Ronald Reagan sagely observed, "Our people look for a cause to believe in. Is it a third party we need, or is it a new and revitalized second party, raising a banner of no pale pastels, but bold colors which make it unmistakably clear where we stand on all of the issues troubling the people." America is itself a red, white, and blue bold-colored solution to many around the world yearning for a place to secure their unalienable rights. Our government works best when we focus upon securing our rights to life, liberty, and the pursuit of happiness rather than focus upon giving up these rights for pale-pastel solutions that give a semblance of security.

Michigan has recovered from the Lost Decade but we have many lost opportunities that could have made our recovery even stronger. I've outlined some of these opportunities in this chapter along with a glimpse into solutions that could make the government more efficient and effective and help to restore respect in our public servants. My proposed solutions are not just any solutions, though. I offer bold, principled solutions that push back against the orthodoxy of the Swamp, with a "fix it" manual for many of the most common problems faced by state government.

My campaign literature and other materials feature the simple description: "A Problem Solver, Not a Politician." It is more than a slogan. It is how I operate. One of the most troubling aspects of how Lansing and many other government bodies operate is that most problems feature only one solution. You either get on board with that solution or you don't. In my background, I was trained to recognize that there are often multiple solutions to a given problem. When I was an instructor at Space Camp, I taught students how to conduct engineering trade studies to determine the optimum solution to a given problem. In short, the legislature gives true or false quizzes when they should be giving multiple-choice quizzes—although often they give long essay responses that get us nowhere.

The solutions I am sharing are not promoted by any lobbying groups. This is not the norm. They were developed after an exhaustive examination of the respective problems and a sincere desire to find the best solution for the people we serve. And they all comply with the guidelines and constraints of our Constitution. Not only did I develop these solutions, but I also did the unthinkable. I promoted them without the blessing of the folks in control of the Swamp. The unwritten rule is that I am supposed to sit back and simply vote no.

Have you ever proposed a solution to a problem only to have someone say, "That's impossible. It'll never work"? I have. Perhaps that is what motivated me to go into aerospace engineering. Nothing motivates me more than for someone to tell me it is impossible.

At one time in history, nothing seemed more impossible than human beings taking flight. At one time in history, nothing seemed more impossible than landing a man on the moon and returning him safely back to Earth. America is the land of making the impossible, possible I'm not just talking about the Wright Brothers. I'm not just talking about Neil Armstrong and my former professor at the International Space University, Buzz Aldrin. Millions of everyday Americans from all walks of life routinely do what many politicians in government today believe to be impossible. Government officials often make excuses why something can't be done while everyday Americans find ways to get it done. That alone is a pretty good argument for term limits.

I grow tired of people who say something can't be done. I have learned that when someone says that something can't be done, all they are really saying is "I don't want it to happen" or "I don't want to do it that way."

For the sake of our citizens, I say it is about time that we started to consider actually doing the impossible.

It is time to establish some Big Harry Audacious Goals or BHAGs.

There is an old adage that goes like this: "People who say it cannot be done should not interrupt those who are doing it."

I'm tired of being interrupted and so are citizens across America.

## HEALTH CARE
### Problem

Simply put, health care in America costs too much and provides too little care in return. Deductibles on insurance plans are so high that many wonder why they have insurance at all. This high cost impairs access to health care for all of us, but it hits the poor hardest of all.

How do we improve access to low cost, high quality health care? The federal government's response to this question was HR 3590 commonly known as Obamacare and otherwise known as the Patient-Protection and Affordable Care Act (PPACA). After reading this law, it was clear to me that this legislation not only does not protect patients, it is also not affordable and not caring. The only truth in the title is that it is an act. In reality, the PPACA is about *control*.

Shortly after my decision to run for office, on the morning of March 22, 2010, I was working out in the basement while listening to the Paul W Smith Show on WJR in Detroit. Paul W asked his guest, Congressman John Dingell, why it was going to take four years to implement Obamacare when, by his own figures, seventy-two thousand Americans were dying each year due to lack of health care. Congressman Dingell responded as follows:

> Let me remind you this [Americans allegedly dying because of lack of universal health care] has been going on for years. We are bringing it to a halt. The harsh fact of the matter is when you're going to pass legislation that will cover 300 [million] American people in different ways it takes a long time to do the necessary administrative steps that have to be taken to put the legislation together to *control the people*.

That certainly was clear confirmation to me as to what the law was really about. Remember, this is the same legislation about which President Obama repeatedly said, "If you like your insurance, you can keep your insurance." Or "If you like your doctor, you can keep your doctor." At least Congressman Dingell was truthful.

You may be wondering why a state legislator is concerned with federal legislation.

First of all, Article IV Section 51 of the Michigan Constitution, which I swore an oath to support makes it my concern: "The public health and general welfare of the people of the state are hereby declared to be matters of primary public concern. The legislature shall pass suitable laws for the protection and promotion of the public health."

Second of all, since our US Constitution, which I also swore an oath to support, grants no such authority to the federal government within the enumerated powers of Article I Section 8 of our US Constitution, the federal government has no business messing with the health care policies of any state, including Michigan. And the federal government has done a lot of messing with state health care policies. Among the more harmful of these messes that state legislatures need to clean up are the following:

- Certificate of Need (aka Health Planning Resources Development Act of 1974)
- State-Based Exchanges (aka Section 1314 of HR 3590)
- Medicaid Expansion (aka Section 2001 of HR 3590)

Third of all, it turns out that good health care policy is the lynch pin for solving quite a few other problems faced by states.

### Solution

The key to expanding access to health care is to lower the cost of providing quality health care not subsidizing the cost of care for some at the expense of others. Yet little energy seems to be devoted to reducing the cost of health care. Why is that? Most of the folks lobbying for health care reform are the folks who benefit from higher costs in health care. They key to breaking the cycle of ever-increasing health care costs is to prevent these lobbyists from driving the health care debate. Special interests only result in protectionist policies that hurt consumers. We need free market reforms, and we need them badly.

Throughout the battle against a state-based health exchange and Medicaid expansion, I promoted the need for free market health care solutions. We needed to get the government out from between a doctor and patient. Early on, my focus was on removing regulatory barriers and promoting competition. One night, that all changed.

I was watching a segment of *Huckabee* on the Fox News Channel that featured a trio of doctors talking about something that I had never heard of before: direct primary care (DPC). The next day I called the offices of each of the doctors who appeared on *Huckabee* to dig for more information on DPC. I received a call back from Dr. Josh Umbehr, a doctor in Wichita. In a phone call that lasted at least forty-five minutes he explained to me how DPC worked and how, when used in conjunction with self-insured plans, he had saved his clients up to 50 percent in annual health care costs while receiving better coverage. We were instant friends. Dr. Josh is now a regular guest on *Hannity* talking about DPC. Josh later put me in contact with his business guru, Joe Martin, who filled me in on all of the legalese that made DPC possible during the age of Obamacare. Joe has also become a great friend. It was clear that DPC was the free market ace-in-the-hole that I had been looking for. DPC fundamentally changes the health care debate. Instead of focusing on who would get stuck with the bill for ever-increasing health care costs, we finally had a way to expand access to quality health care by *reducing* costs.

So what exactly is direct primary care?

Before I explain direct primary care, let's look at the background on health plans. In today's market, a health plan consists of two basic components: primary care and catastrophic care. Primary care involves mostly routine, affordable care that is provided by a primary care physician like a pediatrician, internist, or family practice physician. Catastrophic care is required when a patient is faced with a serious chronic illness or accident requiring hospitalization. Catastrophic care is significantly more expensive than primary care. Eighty percent of insurance transactions pertain to primary care.

Health insurance used to be focused on catastrophic care. In fact, it used to be focused upon managing the risks of expensive hospital stays or chronic illnesses. As Dr. Umbehr likes to say, you wouldn't pay for gas fill-ups or oil changes with your auto insurance would you? No. Auto insurance is reserved for expensive events like car accidents or thefts. Don't use it for your oil changes. Over the past couple of decades, however, health insurance has become health management not risk management. Now there are quite a few administrative layers between a doctor and a patient for both primary and catastrophic care. In fact, under Obamacare, 159 new organizations were added that get between a doctor and patient to regulate health plans for all citizens whether they need government assistance or not. Does the addition of 159 new organizations that come between a doctor and a patient seem more affordable to you?

Direct primary care allows doctors and patients to tell these 159 organizations to "talk to the hand." The keyword in direct primary care is *direct*. DPC effectively eliminates the middleman for routine health-care services and refocuses health care on the doctor-patient relationship.

The good news is that in order to get the necessary votes for passage, Obamacare included a loophole that protects DPCS. It turns out that Section 10104 of Obamacare authorizes the use of direct primary care medical home plans as components of a qualified health plan under Section 1301 of HR 3590. Without this loophole, Obamacare would have effectively enshrined "health management" not "risk management" as the purpose of all insurance policies, leaving no room for free-market solution such as DPCS.

How does DPC reduce costs?

First all, it removes all of the regulations promoted by the government and insurance bureaucracies between a doctor and a patient. Among the most time-consuming of these regulations is something called Current Procedural Terminology or CPT coding. Did you ever wonder why your doctor walks into the waiting room with a laptop or tablet? In order for doctors to get paid, they need to apply the correct code for a given patient visit in the Electronic Medical Record (EMR) system. These codes are captured in the invoice sent to the insurance companies. The codes are cataloged in the International Classification of Diseases, Tenth Revision, Clinical Modification (ICD-10-CM) or International Classification of Diseases, Tenth Revision, Procedure Coding System (ICD-10-PCS).

There are sixty-eight thousand ICD-10-CM codes and eighty-seven thousand ICD-10-PCS codes. Examples of these codes[1] include:

> W51.XXXA: Accidental striking against or bumped into by another person, initial encounter.
> W61.12XA: Struck by macaw, initial encounter.
> R46.1: Bizarre personal appearance.
> R46.2 Strange and inexplicable behavior.
> R46.3 Overactivity.

My personal favorites as an aerospace engineer are:

> V97.33XD: Sucked into jet engine, subsequent encounter.
> W22.02XD: V95.43XS: Spacecraft collision injuring occupant, sequela.

Melvil Dewey eat your heart out!

Please note that these codes go beyond describing specific conditions to specifying how these conditions were achieved. This is the difference between health management and health care. All of this data will be tabulated and used as the justification for government-mandated behavioral modifications that might lower health care costs. It also provides a pretty good supplement to any behavioral profile that the government might have on any individual citizen. Upon reading every page of Obamacare, I was convinced that it was all about control not care. Coding systems like this provide ample evidence of this assertion.

Did you ever wonder why the American Medical Association supported Obamacare? As it turns out, they had 72 million reasons.

As the owner of the CPT-code set, they received $72 million from "royalties and credentialing products" in 2010.[2] During that same year, they only received $38 million in membership dues.

Insurance-based primary care practices require a team of back office support personnel to manage the accounts receivable with insurance companies. Direct primary care practices often operate without any back-office personnel. Doctors in insurance-based practices spend almost half of their time on administrative duties related to the third-party payment model. DPC docs get paid on the basis of monthly subscription fees. No third-party system coding is required. Instead, they get to focus their precious time on you, the patient. This translates to another important way that DPC practices lower costs: preventive care. It is not unusual for DPC docs to spend a half an hour or more with a single patient—especially for first time visits. When was the last time that you spent thirty minutes of quality time with your primary care physician? The more time that a doctor spends with a patient on preventive care the less likely the patient is to need expensive catastrophic care. In other words, patients receive improved access to the relatively low-cost care provided by primary care physicians so as to keep them out of expensive specialist or hospital visits. In short, DPC provides better care for less money—on average more than 20 percent less.[3] Yet the march towards health management insurance rather than the traditional role of risk management continues.

The only way to stop health management insurance and protect DPC practices from government or insurance industry regulations is through legislation. We need a bill that simply says that DPC agreements shall not be treated as insurance products.

I went on to pass DPC legislation with this provision plus transparency provisions regarding DPC agreements in Michigan. Public Act 522 was signed into law in 2014. And I am pleased to say that at the time of my writing this book, eighteen states have passed similar laws.

Michigan is seeing rapid growth in direct primary care providers in the wake of the passage of my bill. An estimated 150 doctors have already adopted the direct primary care business model in the state of Michigan and more are contacting my office as word spreads. Direct primary care is good for doctors, good for patients, and good for employers seeking quality health care options for their employees.

I like to refer to DPC as a free market loophole in Obamacare through which I would like to drive a Mack truck. DPC was around before Obamacare, and it will be along well after Obamacare is confined to the ash heap of history.

I am now in full evangelism mode. For more information on DPC, please see DPCFrontier.org or DPCare.org.

Now, if you wish to keep IRS agents from knocking on your door because you do not have an Obamacare "Qualified Health Plan," you need more than a DPC agreement. You need to have an insurance policy or "health ministry" that fills the coverage gap between the scope of your DPC contract and the minimum essential benefits defined in Obamacare.

At the time of writing, neither Medicaid nor Medicare allow for direct reimbursement of DPC services. Plus, most traditional insurance providers do not yet offer health plans that do not include primary care services coverage, so you would essentially be paying twice for such services when you have a DPC agreement.

The best options for wraparound coverage to complement a DPC agreement would be self-insured plans, multi-employer welfare arrangements (MEWAS), or health care sharing ministries such as Christian Medi-Share. Employers who have pursued these DPC-compatible solutions have seen savings on the order of 30 to 60 percent without sacrificing quality of care.[4]

Even for expensive surgeries there is a cash-only business model that works and is exemplified by the Surgery Center of Oklahoma founded by Dr. Doug Smith. When insurance deductibles reach the $5,000 or $10,000 threshold, the value of paying insurance premiums comes into question. The Surgery Center of Oklahoma provides the answer to this question using a pricing guide that in some cases are 90 percent less than what it cost under traditional insurance. Say good-bye to hospital bills featuring $1300 for eye drops or $300 for an aspirin. Go to surgerycenterok.com to see transparent pricing on surgical procedures simply by selecting the part of the body requiring surgery.

In a nutshell, free market health care solutions like DPC plus self-insured plans return the purpose of insurance back to risk management and away from overarching health management.

In addition to DPC fixing health care, it can also be used to solve other problems faced by government. In fact, I like to refer to DPC as government's Swiss army knife because one tool, DPC, can do so much. Remember, government is one big professional service firm. Professional service firms employee a lot of people. People need health care. The savings from DPC-based health plans could be used to fix the roads, fill budget potholes, stretch school dollars, free up more resources for local government, and lower auto insurance costs, among other things.

How could DPC help fix our government policy potholes?

We spend $664 million per year to provide health insurance for over fifty-one thousand state employees. A 20 percent savings frees up $133 million per year. We spend $18 billion per year on Medicaid for over 2.4 million citizens. A 20 percent savings frees up $3.6 billion per year, of which almost $1.4 billion comes from state revenue. We spend $1.25 billion per year on health care costs in education. A 20 percent savings frees up $250 million per year, or over $167 per pupil. We spend an estimated $775 million per year on local government health care. A 20 percent savings frees up $155 million per year for our communities to hire more policemen and firemen. Each of us spends almost $2,000 per vehicle per year on no-fault auto insurance in Michigan. Health care services account for almost 70% of the cost of Michigan's no-fault insurance. A 20 percent savings should reduce the cost of no-fault insurance by up to $280 per vehicle per year. A reduction of 20 percent in the liabilities for the current $20 billion Michigan Catastrophic Claims Association Fund would free up $4 billion for further reductions in insurance premiums. Last but not least, Michigan businesses spend an estimated $35 billion per year on health care. A 20 percent savings frees up $7 billion per year for employers to invest in their employees and help their business achieve a competitive edge over businesses in other states. This would have a tremendous impact on job growth in Michigan. This job growth would in turn generate additional tax revenue to fill all of the potholes previously cited simply by getting more people back to work.

Do you know what the best feature of this solution is? The way that government saves taxpayer money is by delivering better services and making people *healthier*!

In short, direct primary care could be used as a "Swiss army knife" to fix many of the policy issues facing state governments as well as our federal government. As we expand the use of this tool, we have an opportunity for a free market revolution in health care. This revolution will reverse today's trend towards less care and more money to one that provides better care for less money. Now, isn't that a worthy pursuit?

## EDUCATION
### Problem

Within the halls of Lansing and many other state capitols around the nation, the purpose of education is touted as to develop students who are "college and career ready." This is a far cry from the purpose of education enshrined in our Michigan Constitution that actually produced some of the most remarkable college and career ready students the world has ever known. The Michigan Constitution starts off the section on education with the following statement on the purpose of education, "Religion, morality and knowledge being necessary to good government and the happiness of mankind, schools and the means of education shall forever be encouraged." Per our Michigan Constitution therefore, the purpose of education is to foster good government via the development of moral, religious, and knowledgeable citizens. It should be noted for those who espouse the fallacy that our Founders believed in freedom *from* religion doctrine that these words come straight from the first piece of legislation passed under our new Constitution, The Northwest Ordinance of 1787.

In today's public schools, religion is outlawed (at least Christianity) and morality is often limited to various prefixes to the word justice. Nebulous terms such as restorative justice, distributive justice, social justice, racial justice, and environmental justice have replaced traditional moral values such as being trustworthy, loyal, helpful, friendly, courteous, kind, obedient, cheerful, thrifty, brave, clean, and reverent. Is it any wonder why the homeschool movement in Michigan is one of the strongest in the country? Sadly, not even knowledge is a principle objective ever since Michigan's State Board of Education adopted the Common Core standards for math and language arts on June 15, 2010. Under Common Core, students can get the wrong answer but still get kudos for adhering to the correct process.

One of the most concerning features of the Common Core Standards is the increase in emphasis on methods at the expense of correctness. The following is an example of the math standard for first graders:

> Add and subtract within 20, demonstrating fluency for addition and subtraction within 10. Use strategies such as counting on; making ten (e.g., $8 + 6 = 8 + 2 + 4 = 10 + 4 = 14$); decomposing a number leading to a ten (e.g., $13 - 4 = 13 - 3 - 1 = 10 - 1 = 9$); using the relationship between addition and subtraction (e.g., knowing that $8 + 4 = 12$, one knows $12 - 8 = 4$); and creating equivalent but easier or known sums (e.g., adding $6 + 7$ by creating the known equivalent $6 + 6 + 1 = 12 + 1 = 13$)."

Note that the standard emphasizes the methodology used not that the student gets the correct answer. If you were a passenger on an airplane experiencing severe turbulence, would you be more concerned that the aerospace engineer who designed the aircraft calculated the correct design properties to keep the plane flightworthy or that the engineer knew of four different ways to perform the calculations? The growing disdain for raw knowledge in the era of "Google it" is concerning to say the least. As a techie, even I know that sometimes real-life decisions need to be made away from an internet connection.

Perhaps the best way to understand Common Core is to understand how our education system is organized. I developed Figure 7 during my time serving on the Michigan Senate Education Policy Committee.

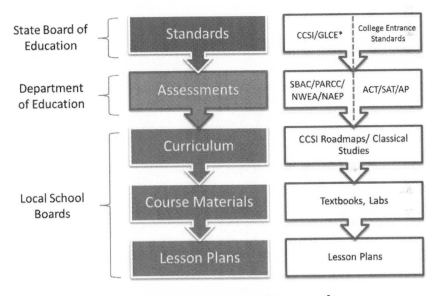

*Figure 7: Education System Framework*

There is an overwhelming trend against local control and towards more and more centralized control of education. Additional concerns include the increasing role of the federal government in state education. The states lose the ability to influence the governance of its own standards. There is concern over the increasing role of international bodies in the American education system. (International benchmarking is at the heart of each Common Core standard.) There also is growing apprehension as to the cost of implementation, the manipulation of assessments to influence college acceptance criteria, the acceptance of standards before they have even been written, and the collection of data on parents as well as students.

Modifying education standards is not a simple flip of the switch. A change in the education standards requires a change in assessments. A change in assessments leads to changes in curricula. A change in curricula requires a change in education materials. A change in education materials leads to changes in lesson plans.

When I was growing up in the Michigan public school system, we didn't have a statewide assessment. In fact, I don't recall undergoing much standardized testing at all. I do recall taking the California test and Iowa test, but there was no Michigan test. Individual school districts within the state had a certain degree of autonomy from state and federal mandates. As centralized control advocates have grown stronger over the past few decades, their thirst for information to better exercise this control has also grown. As the thirst for information has grown, so has the demand for more and more administrators and support personnel. As more resources are diverted to back office services, fewer resources are available for the classroom.

How successful has this trend towards centralized control of education been?

According to a 2014 Competitiveness Benchmarking Report from the Business Leaders for Michigan, Michigan ranks thirty-eighth in fourth grade reading and thirty-seventh in eighth grade math.

In a recent examination of Michigan students, only 50 percent of third graders were proficient in reading. Only 49 percent of third graders were proficient in math. Only 28 percent were proficient in the eleventh grade. In my Senate district, in the wake of the Lost Decade where citizens struggled to find job openings, we now have more than thirty-one thousand job openings within a thirty-mile radius. The problem? We don't have any graduates qualified to fill these openings yet we have over 230,000 people unemployed in our state workforce.[5]

Exacerbating our performance woes is the continued tension between public school academies (aka charter schools) and traditional public schools. Why? Public school academies (PSAs) are predominantly non-union. Traditional public schools are union. At a time when we should be focused upon the best interests of our kids, too many in the education community are focused instead on what is in the presumed best interest of adults.

Michigan spends over $14.7 billion annually on public education. That amount is second only to our Medicaid budget of $18.6 billion. And during my short tenure in the Senate, spending on education in Michigan has increased by almost $1.2 billion, but so have the number of controls placed upon that spending.

The pension system for public school employees in Michigan is known as MPSERS (Michigan Public School Employee Retirement System). Prior to reforms enacted in 2012, the pension system promised an 8 percent return on all investments made by employees and the state on behalf of the employees. The problem with that is that the actual return was only 2.9 percent over the previous three years and only 5 percent for the previous ten years. Guess who had to make up the difference between expectations and the reality of the market during the Lost Decade? You guessed it: taxpayers. It turns out that the lion's share of that $1.2 billion increase needed to go to MPSERS to ensure its solvency. If MPSERS were not solvent, retired school employees would be very disappointed when they attempted to draw down on their accounts. The allocation of over $1 billion to shore up MPSERS resulted in cries for more funding to schools.

### Solution

The key to fixing public education is centered on funding but not necessarily in the way many in the public education bureaucracy think. They would have you believe that spending more money on public education is the answer. Perhaps that is the case, and indeed I have ways to do so without raising taxes, but I would submit that it more important to discuss *how* we spend our money before determining whether or not we are spending enough. In keeping with my time-tested governance principles, we need to promote more first-party transactions. Parents and students need to be in the driver's seat. This may sound like simply another politician platitude, but it's not.

As a member of the Senate Education Committee, I have been privy to what works and what doesn't work when it comes to education reform. On the basis of statewide assessments required by the federal government, Michigan's School Reform Office (SRO), which was implemented prior to my tenure in the Michigan state legislature, issued notices to thirty-eight "priority schools" across the state, marking them for closure due to poor performance. There is no doubt the schools were struggling; whether closure would be the best course of action remains to be seen. In response to the SRO notice, Senator Phil Pavlov, chair of the Senate Education Policy Committee introduced SB 27, which would repeal the 2010 law that formed the SRO. In order to evaluate the potential impact of the proposed bill, the committee heard more than three months' worth of testimony that featured proposals for school accountability systems that might replace the SRO as well as a discussion of methods that have been proven to turnaround low-performance schools. We heard testimony from superintendents, principals, the Michigan Department of Education, a state school board member, the Education Achievement Authority, the School Reform Office, community groups, teachers, students, lobbyists, think tanks, lawyers, and turnaround consultants.

I listened intently to all the stakeholders who testified. I took notes. And the conclusions were fairly obvious. It was clear from the testimony that the higher the accountability authority, the more onerous the accountability system (See Figure 8). For example, if the accountability authority is the federal government, the requirements include not only standardized tests, such as Smarter Balance or PARCC, to determine school performance but also a plethora of additional information as outlined in the Department of Education Longitudinal Data System on top of any information needed by the state, intermediate school districts, local school boards, principals, or teachers in the classroom. On the opposite end spectrum would be an accountability system that cuts out all the layers of bureaucracy and is limited to teachers evaluating individual student performance and reporting their assessment to the parents of the student.

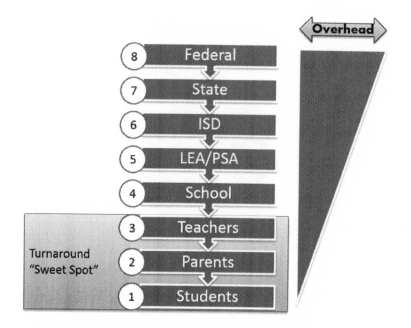

*Figure 8: Education Accountability Levels*

Everyone who testified seemed to agree on the desired attributes of any new accountability system, which included: local control, clear expectation management, flexibility, choice, and low administrative burden.

It was also evident from the testimony that the keys to turning low performance schools into high performance schools are teachers, parents and students who bond together and declare "not on my watch" in both words and action. The state could facilitate such action, but any attempt by the state to mandate such action would not be successful without the support of teachers, parents, and students.

So how does this translate into effective education policy?

First, we need to respect the desire for local control, clearly manage expectations, be flexible in our policies, offer more choice, and lower the administrative burden by restoring the role of the federal and state governments to their constitutional boundaries. Since the federal government has no enumerated power regarding education policy, the Federal Department of Education should be eliminated. That also means that national policies such as the Common Core Standards Initiative have no place in our nation's education system. It should be repealed in all of its forms. Furthermore, since the constitutional role of state government is limited to that of encouraging education and providing for a free system of public education, the state department of education and state board of education should resume focusing on such matters rather than bathroom policy and promoting man-made global warming nonsense.

Second, we need to implement education-funding policies that provide choice, are sustainable, and match funding to the need. In other words, we need to promote the first-party transaction model in education. It turns out there is a way to accomplish this objective while also freeing up over three thousand dollars per pupil per year for education *without* raising taxes. How can this be achieved? The answer is education savings accounts.

In order to better understand how education savings accounts (ESA) would work in practice, let's take a closer look at the Detroit Public School (DPS) system. In 2016, DPS was bankrupt. Years of mismanagement and outright corruption resulted in over $617 million in debt. There were forty-seven thousand students in DPS who were struggling to get access to a quality education. The state ended up passing a bailout package that ultimately took money from other state funding priorities to address the insolvency of DPS. ESAs would have provided a means of meeting these debt obligations without draining funds that could have been used for roads or health care or public safety.

Detroit Public Schools were not the only unit of government in Detroit. The city itself was the subject of the largest municipal bankruptcy in history. The full impact of the bankruptcy was mitigated via a bailout package that featured significant non-government funding sources. The primary interest of these non-government benefactors was not the city so much as it was one of the most valued assets of the city: the Detroit Institute of Arts (DIA). Non-government sources contributed $300 million to the bailout package spurred on by the desire to protect this generational asset. It was an example of government officials looking beyond tax increases to solve a problem.

So let's find a way to promote non-government funding sources for education.

Student-specific ESAs open the door to private sector contributors who have a vested interest in the success of an individual student. Contributors to ESAs might include prospective employers struggling to find qualified workers, philanthropic foundations, or consumer loyalty program participants interested in directing their loyalty awards to a specific student or group of students.

In order to erase the DPS debt, the state needed only fifteen hundred dollars per student per year for the next ten years. Parochial schools in Detroit are already operating with third-party contributions of seven thousand dollars per year per student in exchange for work-study arrangements that benefit students and employers alike. Loyalty programs are an $80 billion market nationwide, opening the door to contributions of one thousand dollars or more into ESAs. Foundations are yet another source of private funding.

The state simply needs to implement a mechanism for these organizations to contribute in a way that is specific to an individual student. Educational Savings Accounts provide that mechanism. Plus, it is important to note that that ESAs would help solve funding issues well beyond a single K-12 school system like DPS. Do you think that DPS is the only education institution seeking additional funding? What about students struggling with the high cost of college education? How about current members of the workforce seeking additional training or professional development? ESAs provide a way to address these issues too—*without* raising taxes.

Why do ESAs work? Student-specific education savings accounts promote first-party transactions. Parents and students are able to shop for the best education value for their money. The current education funding model features third-party transactions where bureaucrats are paid to provide education services for students they may or may not know. With ESAs, parents, *not bureaucrats*, would direct how that money is spent.

We have much more work to do, but the secret is not much of a secret at all. It's time to refocus education upon parents, teachers, and students.

### Energy

Energy is the lifeblood of our economy and central to the quality of life that we enjoy in America.

### Problem

How do we provide consumers with access to low-cost, sustainable, and reliable energy?

The current energy market in Michigan is heavily regulated. In fact, 90 percent of the market is under the control of regulated utilities. The remaining 10 percent consists of what is referred to as the "electric choice market." Customers in the choice market, which include many of our school systems, claim cost savings up to 20 percent. A report conducted for Compete, a coalition of electricity stakeholders, cites that the fourteen competitive states increased cost of electricity by 40.9 percent between 1997 and 2014 while monopoly states increased costs by 59.9 percent.[6]

One of the problems with our current energy market is that there are no downward cost pressures on utilities. There is no motivation for them to improve the efficiency of their operations in a manner that benefits consumers. Price fluctuations reflect fluctuations in commodity prices for any consumables such as coal or natural gas needed to supply the state's electricity needs. The push for sustainable energy sources has resulted in significant investments in wind turbines and solar facilities throughout our state. Since the wind is not constant and solar cells do not work well at night when many of our homes experience peak demand, these energy sources still need to be supplemented by a base load capacity from consumable energy sources such as natural gas and coal.

Under pressure from state and federal government agencies, utilities have launched programs that promote conservation. Our consumers receive energy report cards that track our energy usage relative to our neighbors.

I support conservation, but I question the methods that the utility companies promote. After all, these publicly traded companies make money on the basis of how much electricity they sell. Why would they aggressively promote programs that discourage the use of their product? That would be like an auto manufacturer promoting the use of bicycles instead of cars.

As it turns out, utilities in Michigan make money from much more than selling electricity. Much like how the insurance companies were protected against significant losses in exchange for their support of Obamacare, utilities are protected by the government against losses for capital investments they might make toward improving the reliability of our power grid. Sounds reasonable right?

Unfortunately, as instituted in Michigan, this strategy incentivizes utilities to spend more and more on capital investments whether or not they benefit the consumer. How so? you might ask. In addition to receiving consumer electricity rate adjustments to hold utilities harmless on capital investments, utilities derive more than a 10 percent return on equity from these investments. How do they generate more revenue? Simply by injecting more capital investment projects into their company project portfolio.

In short, energy utilities could provide zero kilowatts per hour of electricity and still make more than 10 percent return on equity from their capital investments. This effectively converts our energy utilities into bond fund management companies.

Another problem area pertains to the implementation of so-called smart grid technology. It has been sold as a way to improve the network efficiency of our nation's electric grids and arm consumers with information that would allow them to be more cost conscious with their energy use. In reality, this "smart grid" has been demonstrated to actually increase our vulnerability to bad actors.

Furthermore, smart meters installed at homes and apartments not only collect data that potentially infringes upon Fourth

Amendment rights, they also have been linked to health concerns for certain segments of the population. Electric companies threaten to shut off power to customers who refuse installation of these smart meters. In fact, constituents in my district who prefer their analog meters to smart meters are treated much worse than customers who are unable to pay their electric bill. It reeks of a control issue rather than looking out for the best interests of consumers.

Another peculiarity in Michigan's energy market is that regulated utilities spend millions of dollars every year on advertising campaigns, yet with 90 percent of the market, they are virtual monopolies. Why do they need to spend any money on advertising? After all, everyone already knows who they are. As it turns out, advertising money goes to radio, TV, and print businesses that are the same ones who cover politics and the various policy debates. In light of the media's dependence upon these ad dollars, how likely do you think it is that these outlets will cover any stories that might threaten these virtual monopolies?

### *Solution*

In today's society energy ranks right up there with food and water in terms of necessity. In fact, without reliable access to energy, life as we know it simply shuts down. There is no question that access to reliable energy is important for all of us. How can we best ensure safe and affordable access?

Promote energy choice and let consumers drive demand for renewable energy stewardship.

If a consumer wants wind energy, then they should pay the market rate on wind energy. If a consumer wants solar energy, they should be able to pay the market rate on solar energy. If a consumer wants hydro energy, they should be able to pay the market rate on hydro energy. If a consumer wants to purchase the lowest cost energy, they should be able to purchase low-cost energy. If a consumer does not want a smart meter on their home, they should not be forced to have a smart meter on their home.

The future of electricity is not in complex, capital intensive statewide electrical grids. The future of electricity is in microgrids. A microgrid generally operates alongside the main grid, but it can break off and operate on its own using local energy generation in times of crisis like storms or power outages, or for other reasons. A microgrid can be powered by distributed generators, batteries, and/or renewable resources. Conservation efforts would be more localized, rather than Big Brother monitoring energy consumption. Improved battery performance has been a disrupter in the energy market. Solar and wind technologies have long suffered from highly unreliable energy availability. No sun, no power. No wind, no power. Batteries help fill the gaps in sunshine and wind. Innovative technologies such as those promoted by Tesla and Bloom Energy offer the potential to make traditional large-scale power plants obsolete, which provides all the more reason to question the public benefit of providing utilities with guaranteed high rates of returns for capital investments.

Microgrids are less vulnerable to power grid security threats, especially cyber threats. Our enemies would need to deactivate more than a few extremely high voltage substations and supervisory control and data acquisition systems, or SCADAS, to cut the power to our communities.

Let me be clear. Government does not create jobs. Government can only create an environment that encourages job growth.

## JOBS

Government does not create private sector jobs. Government can only create an environment that encourages job growth.

### *Problem*

Job growth is important because a robust jobs market means that families are more likely to have at least one breadwinner in the home to put food on the table. Job growth is not simply all about the money, however. Whenever a state fails to provide an environment that encourages job growth, job opportunities aren't there and families are broken up as family members seek greener pastures in other states.

Job growth is also important because the more people that we have providing for themselves, the fewer people we have dependent upon government programs, which reduces the tax burden on those who are working.

There is another important reason, though, that is often overlooked. Effective job growth policies not only decrease dependence upon government services, it also increases tax revenue *without* increasing tax rates. In fact, for every 1 percent drop in unemployment rate in Michigan, 52,400 workers are paying taxes rather than receiving benefits.

In November 2011, when Michigan's unemployment rate was determined to be 9.8 percent, I asked our Senate Fiscal Agency, all other things being constant, how would our tax revenue change if we were to drop our unemployment rate to 5 percent. The answer? We would add a total of $1.6 billion in tax revenue—subject to a significant number of caveats.

As it turns out, these revenue predictions turned out to be fairly close to reality. I'm happy to say that in January 2016,

Michigan unemployment did indeed drop below 5 percent (to 4.9 percent)[7] so we have a pretty good idea how much tax revenue was actually added.

In 2012, our total budget was $47.5 billion. Our General Fund was $9.5 billion. Our School Aid Fund was $13.3 billion. Our Constitutional Revenue Sharing was $1.0 billion.

In 2016, our total budget was $53.6 billion. Our General Fund was $10.5 billion or $1 billion higher. Our School Aid Fund was $14.3 billion or $1 billion higher. We had $200 million more to spend on police and fire services by local units of government. When adjusted for an ill-conceived tax increase on seniors that accounted for $380 million of increased taxes, a total of $2.2 billion in additional tax revenue was available without increasing tax rates. Pro-growth policies should appeal to both big government advocates and limited government advocates such as myself.

If you want to encourage job growth, wouldn't it make sense to start with an understanding of why employers would seek to hire more employees?

In order to answer that question effectively, I believe it is first necessary to understand what drives a typical business owner to hire somebody. Simply put, it comes down to supply, demand, and financials. Supply and demand are pretty straightforward. If there is a current or projected demand for more work than the current or projected supply of workers can provide, you have a labor gap that would justify hiring additional workers. Before a business owner can hire additional workers, though, it must be financially feasible.

With all the talk of the evils of Big Business and Big Money, it's easy to think that profits are bad, but in reality, profits are actually good. Profit occurs when revenue exceeds expenses. Profits are the difference between staying in business and going out of business. Only when there is sufficient demand and there is confidence in sustained profitability will responsible businesses decide to hire more workers.

For the sake of brevity, let's assume that we have sufficient demand in the market. How do we ensure profitability? We can raise revenue or lower expenses. Let's assume that we have little control over revenue as it is often set by market forces outside of the control of any one business. That leaves us with expenses. What options do we have to lower expenses so as to increase profitability?

One of the most common ways that states attempt to lower these costs is to fund quasi-government entities called Economic Development Corporations. More often than not these organizations assume the role of venture capitalists that risk taxpayer money as capital on their ventures. Approximately $1 billion of Michigan's $56 billion state budget is spent annually on such ventures. These organizations use grants, low-interest loans, and tax abatements to incentivize a business of interest to locate or expand their operations in the state. In practice, it leads to situations where the taxes paid by a business and their employees could actually be used to subsidize the costs for one of their competitors.

The good news is that the proponents of these economic development corporations recognize that lower costs result in job growth. The bad news is that they only assist businesses with sufficient political muscle to qualify for such subsidies. There must be a better, fairer way to incentivize economic growth. The good news is that there is.

### Solutions

The key to governments creating better, fairer environments for job growth is to first realize that under our system of government, policies are supposed to yield equal benefit for all of our citizens. In fact, the Michigan Constitution unequivocally states that "Government is instituted for [the] equal benefit, security and protection [of the people]." This means that elected officials should avoid the temptation of "quick fix" policies that benefit a specific high-profile business prospect or industry and pursue instead what I refer to as a "broad-based economic development policy." A broad-based economic development strategy features sustainable, long-term policies that benefit all businesses in the state. In order to do this effectively, we need to get back to job growth basics—lowering the total cost of business operations expense by expense.

How does this broad-based approach compare to targeted economic development incentives? Let's take a look at one of the incentive programs recently implemented in Michigan for the growing data center industry. Truth be told, it started out as a program designed for a single data center but was later broadened to most data centers in order to get a sufficient number of votes to pass the pertinent legislation.

Typical expense line items for data centers would include taxes, electricity, and health care. It turns out that every day citizens also pay for taxes, electricity, and health care.

What if we were to lower the total cost of doing business by adopting policies that lower taxes, lower the cost of health care, and lower the costs of monopolistic utility rates? Not only would we encourage the growth of businesses, more important we would also lighten the financial load on our families.

How would a broad-based economic development policy replace something like the $11 million-a-year data center program? Let's look at how much money data center companies spend on electricity. Data centers have high electricity demands. Electricity is required to power up computers and cool them down. A typical data center has electric bills of $9.5 million per year.[8] If the state were to adopt policies such as real electric choice, we could reduce the cost of electricity by more than 10 percent across the state.[9] That would result in potential savings of $54.5 million per year for the same data centers that would otherwise be eligible for the $11 million state incentive program,[10] In contrast with the data center program, though, electric choice would also result in an average annual electricity cost savings of $127 for every family in the state.[11]

Let's look at how much money the data center would spend on health care for its employees. A minimum of four hundred jobs must be created for the data center program to continue past 2022. The cost of health care for four hundred employees is roughly $7.3 million per year.[12] A savings of 20 percent on health care costs would save them over $1.4 million per year.[13] These same reductions in health care expenses would save the average family in Michigan $3,628 per year.[14]

Another opportunity to lower the cost of doing business for the majority of small businesses is to eliminate the state personal income tax. Doing so in Michigan would shave another 4.25 percent off of the bottom line and save money on CPA time. You know who else benefits? You guessed it. Michigan families would also see an effective 4.25 percent pay raise plus more time with the family around tax time.

In summary, a broad-based economic development strategy would have yielded $55.9 million in savings for the data center industry. Even if this estimate is off four-fold, data centers would still see more savings through a broad-based incentive program than a state program that picks winners and losers. Furthermore, the state's data center program saved Michigan families $0. A broad-based economic development strategy would have saved Michigan families over $3,755 per year.

So, we could grow our state's economy by way of targeted tax incentives to favored businesses or we could adopt policies that not only would help businesses but also help families struggling to make ends meet. I acknowledge that it is much more difficult to pursue broad-based policies. It can be quite challenging to reduce health care costs, reduce electricity costs, or lower taxes. It is much easier to simply carve out $1 billion from a $56 billion budget to place a bet using taxpayer money on a business with the ear of the power brokers in government. The easy way is not always the best way. I believe that this challenge has many parallels with the challenge that President John F. Kennedy issued regarding landing a man on the moon and returning him safely back to the earth by the end of the decade:

> We choose to go to the Moon in this decade and do the other things, not because they are easy, but because they are hard; because that goal will serve to organize and measure the best of our energies and skills, because that challenge is one that we are willing to accept, one we are unwilling to postpone, and one we intend to win.[15]

It is my hope that legislators across the nation will pursue economic development policies that may be hard, but in the end, we all win.

## ELECTION INTEGRITY

The principle of one citizen, one vote must be preserved.

### *Problem*

The November 8, 2016, presidential election in Michigan was very close. Donald Trump won the state by a mere ten thousand votes out of a total of 2.4 million votes cast. Jill Stein, the Green Party presidential candidate, asked for a recount in Michigan even though she had garnered less than 1 percent of the vote. It was clearly done as a mea culpa on behalf of a philosophically aligned Hillary Clinton. Clinton would have won Michigan if only 11,613 of the 50,700 votes earned by Jill Stein would have gone instead to Clinton.

Jill Stein's call for a recount revealed several cracks in the integrity of our election process. One of the most notable "cracks" was the fact that 59 percent of Detroit's 662 precincts[16] would not be subject to a recount because the physical ballot count did not match the voter count in the precinct poll books. My district manager, Penny Crider, was present for the recount preparation for one of these precincts. In Precinct 152, the poll book said that there were 305 votes in the precinct yet when the sealed container holding the ballots was opened, there were only fifty ballots in the box. To make matters worse, Detroit poll results featured 782 more votes than voters.

In response, I initiated a letter to the state attorney general and secretary of state asking for an investigation into voting irregularities. The secretary of state responded to the letter by launching an audit of the election. The audit featured two primary investigations. One thread examined electronic poll book entries against data in the qualified voter file. The examination revealed that there were at least thirty-one incidents of voters voting both at the polls and by way of absentee ballot. Voting more than once is a felony offense. I said at least thirty-one incidents because thirty-three municipalities had yet to submit the information needed by the secretary of state to examine their voting records at the time of the writing of this book. The names of the thirty-one individuals identified as voting twice have been submitted to the Michigan attorney general for further investigation. In the final analysis, the audit did reveal voter fraud. It also revealed the need for better training of election workers.

### Solution

The process of turning this lemon into lemonade is ongoing, but it features a systematic, transparent path to restoring the public trust in the election process. The path to fixing our election process needed to be systematic and transparent. The end goal was to restore faith in our election process. There are key principles that most, if not all, of us would agree are necessary to preserve the integrity of the vote.

### Phase 1: Before One Casts a Vote

- We need to ensure that each citizen is able to vote only once per election
- We need to ensure that the person who casts a ballot is the person registered to cast that ballot
- We need to ensure that only citizens are allowed to vote

### Phase 2: After One Casts a Vote

- We need to ensure that every vote is counted (poll vote and absentee vote, including those of deployed military personnel)

- We need to ensure that every vote is cast only once
- We need to ensure that each vote cast is secured in a manner that makes it plausible to conduct a high integrity recount

Wherever voting irregularities are identified, we need to systematically investigate precinct by precinct in order to determine the root causes of any issues. Where there is negligence, we need an effective corrective action plan that will be monitored by the secretary of state. Where there is a vulnerability in Michigan election law, we need to fill it with appropriate legislation. Where there is outright voter fraud, we need to pursue criminal prosecutions by our attorneys general.

As the vice chair of the Senate Elections and Government Reform Committee, I had taken it upon myself to make sure that I sufficiently understood the current election to make effective policy decisions. In the wake of the audit findings, I decided to kick it up a notch and proceeded to map out our election processes. I evaluated these election processes in much the same way that I performed Failure Modes and Effects Analyses as an engineer with Boeing. The failure modes are ballot count mismatches, more votes than registered voters, and inaccurate votes. The solutions to these failure modes are pretty straightforward. They involve better training. prosecutions to discourage future incidents of voter fraud, and improved transparency. Better training and prosecutions are pretty straightforward. Improved transparency, however, is the key to better election integrity. We need more citizens willing to serve as poll challengers even in precincts where they may not be welcome. If poll challengers are denied access, then we need to have 24/7 video surveillance of all vote control points in the election process monitored by remote poll challengers with access to law enforcement authorities. The integrity of our vote is too precious to turn a blind eye to attempts to subvert it.

## ROADS

Providing our citizens with a safe and reliable transportation infrastructure is in the public interest.

### *Problem*

How do we minimize the cost of maintaining a high-quality transportation infrastructure?

Our state has 252,709 lane-miles in our road system.[17] More than thirty-seven thousand lane-miles of these roads are in poor condition.[18] Every year 4,728 lane-miles of Michigan's roads go from fair to poor at current funding levels.[19] In order to achieve a "sustainable" solution for our roads, we simply need to improve our roads faster than they degrade to "poor" condition. Like many states, Michigan struggles with how best to maintain our transportation infrastructure. Road quality in Michigan is considered to be among the worst in the nation. In fact, our road quality consistently ranks among the ten worst despite spending 53 percent more per mile than the national average.

In Michigan, our transportation budget benchmark is $3.3 billion. Most transportation officials agree that we need an additional $1.2 billion to keep the condition of our current road system from degrading further. In other words, it costs taxpayers $4.5 billion to maintain our state's current transportation system.

The road debate was started by Governor Snyder back in 2011 when he cited it as one of four major issues that we face as a state during his first state of the state address. Only, it really hasn't been much of a debate.

Rather than looking at how *best* we should fix our roads, the objective of the roads debate devolved to how best can we raise at least $1.2 billion to fix our roads. This objective effectively excluded solutions that didn't raise taxes like building higher quality roads and the temporary re-prioritization of existing revenue.

I am committed to fixing our roads. I simply believe that tax increases should only be pursued once all other options have been exhausted.

### Solution

So, what alternatives does Michigan have to raising $1.2 billion in new taxes to maintain our roads?

My mother-in-law actually provided me with the clue to lowering the cost of maintaining our roads. She emigrated from Germany to the United States when she was in her teens. Upon arriving in Michigan, she remarked, "what is going on with all of these orange barrels?" You see, in Germany, they built their roads to last. It led me to investigate exactly how we might be able to make roads last longer in Michigan. Higher quality roads are the lynchpin to lowering total life cycle costs. A nice fringe benefit of roads that last longer is that you see fewer orange barrels.

I spent countless hours searching for data on how to build roads that lasted longer than the twenty-year minimum requirement for Michigan roads. There was surprisingly little data available online. Then I finally came across information on some projects in Ohio and Kentucky that used something called a Cement Hydration Catalyst. I called a company in Michigan called Everlast Concrete Technologies for more information. It turns out that by adding a Cement Hydration Catalyst to the concrete aggregate mix and sealing the pavement after it is poured, Everlast has been able to extend the pavement life by three to four times the base design life. That means that a twenty-year road could last sixty or eighty years. The kicker? Typical government-sponsored long-life road designs simply double the depth of the roadbed, which effectively doubles the construction costs. The Everlast approach, however, only added 15 percent to the sticker price for the entire road project!

Just specifying longer lasting roads won't get you longer lasting roads. We need an accountability system to ensure that the roads truly will last longer. An accountability system for roads, however, is not as simple as slapping on a warranty to a road construction project. There are many variables at play when it comes to ensuring long-lasting roads. One needs to account for each of these variables or else any attempt to enforce warranties will only make trial lawyers rich. One needs to monitor the entire engineering life cycle as well as the assumptions regarding the load cycle to which the roads are subject.

In this spirit, I have introduced legislation in Michigan to require the Michigan Department of Transportation to track the following information for each road project under their supervision:

who designed it,

who built it,

who inspected it,

design life, and

load profile assumptions.

With this information in hand, it will be much easier to identify the cause of any premature road failures as well as enforce extended warranties for the roads.

Better road maintenance techniques are also available for simple pothole maintenance. Many municipalities use Cold Patch repairs or what I call a "throw and roll" technique. A crew of workers tosses out Cold Patch, a ready-made product that is shoveled into the holes and then steamrolled to set it (usually with our car tires). While this product may be easy, there are cost-effective pothole patches—JetPatch and PatchMaster, for instance—that last up to twelve times longer than the life of the standard Cold Patch.

The bottom line is that, if we were to make higher quality roads a priority today, we would eventually need up to $700 million *less* to maintain our roads not $1.2 billion more. It comes down to a discussion of priorities. Tax increases simply push the prioritization discussions from the halls of Lansing to the kitchen tables of our citizens. Legislators need to upgrade our discussions about how to fix the roads and focus on ways to prevent forcing even more of these kitchen table discussions. The key to fixing our nation's crumbling infrastructure is to focus upon building higher quality roads not simply throwing more money at the problem.

We looked at six problems that many states like Michigan are facing: health care, education, energy, jobs, election integrity, and roads. We went beyond defining the problems, though. We defined a suite of bold-colored solutions to these problems. Bold-colored solutions based upon principles are the exceptions not the norm in government. The next chapter illustrates how we can turn these exceptions into the norm.

# 14

# RESTORING FAITH IN GOVERNMENT

It is safe to say that most Americans today are upset about how our government is operating. According to October 2016 polls, 64 percent of Americans believe that America is on the wrong track. Only 28 percent thought we were on the right track. So how do we get on the "right track"?

How do we restore faith in government? It is not a secret. "If my people, who are called by my name, will humble themselves and pray and seek my face and turn from their wicked ways, then will I hear from heaven and will forgive their sin and will heal their land" (2 Chronicles 7:14).

It starts by first restoring our faith in God. Unfortunately, there is a tendency today to put our faith in man.

It seems like we are all looking for a quick fix from an individual. We are looking for the next Reagan. Throughout history, it has been demonstrated that the right leader at the right time can indeed make the difference between a nation surviving and being conveyed to the ash heap of history. While good leadership is very important, it is not what will sustain our nation for the next two hundred years. At most, a new president will help shape the direction of our nation for eight years. That's it.

America is unique among all of the nations of the world in that our nation is governed by the same Constitution today that governed us back in 1789. While we have indeed had many great leaders, no single leader is responsible for that achievement. It is the character of we the people that truly makes the difference. As Alexis de Tocqueville once observed "America is great because she is good. If America ever ceases to be good, she will cease to be great."

## WHAT IS AMERICA'S FORMULA FOR SUCCESS?

As it turns out, our forefathers preserved our formula for success in a little-known monument hidden away in a subdivision in Plymouth, Massachusetts. The National Monument to the Forefathers, also known as the Matrix of Liberty, was designed in 1853 and dedicated on August 1, 1889. It was paid for by the US Congress and the state legislature of Massachusetts. At eighty-one feet in height, it is the largest solid-granite monument in America, and most of us have no idea that it exists. My wife and I didn't when we visited Plymouth, Massachusetts, several years ago. We saw a replica of the Mayflower and Plymouth Rock, but did not have a clue that this monument even existed. The Kirk Cameron movie *Monumental* brought this monument to national attention. We owe him a debt of gratitude for doing so.

Ironically, the monument was established as a *reminder* for how liberty was built in America should we ever lose our way. On it resides the following inscription:

NATIONAL MONUMENT TO THE FOREFATHERS
BY A GRATEFUL PEOPLE IN REMEMBERANCE OF
THEIR LABORS, SACRIFICES AND SUFFERINGS

## FOR THE CAUSE OF CIVIL AND RELIGIOUS LIBERTY

The official description of the monument is as follows:

The monument consists of a forty-five-foot high octagonal shaft of rusticated granite blocks topped by a huge, thirty-six-foot tall female figure representing Faith. Around the base of the shaft are four buttresses each adorned with a seated allegorical figure that represents the principles upon which the Pilgrims founded their commonwealth --Morality, Law, Education, and Liberty. Below the allegorical figures are four reliefs illustrating scenes from the history of the Pilgrims --"Embarkation at Delft Haven," "Signing of the Social Compact in the Cabin of the Mayflower," "Landing at Plymouth," and "First Treaty with the Indians." Small relief figures representing Justice, Mercy, Wisdom, Youth, and Experience are located on the sides of the seated figures. Four recessed arched panels between the seated figures contain inscriptions. On the east panel is the title of the monument and a dedication. The other three panels bear the names of the passenger of the Mayflower.

Faith is a thirty-six-foot high female figure standing at the top of the monument with her proper left foot resting on Plymouth Rock. She holds a copy of the Bible in her proper left hand and she points toward heaven with her raised proper right hand.

On the northeast side at the base of the shaft is a seated
female figure representing Morality. She is dressed in long
robes and in her hands she holds the Decalogue and the
Scroll of Revelation. Below her is a marble relief panel
depicting the Treaty with Massasoit.

On the southeast side at the base of the shaft is a seated
male figure representing Liberty. He is clothed as a
Centurian and in his arms he holds a sword. Beneath his
heel he crushes the chains of bondage. Below him is a
marble relief depicting the Signing of the Compact.
On the southwest side at the base of the shaft is a seated
female figure representing Education. With her proper
right hand she points to a book that she holds in her
proper left hand.

On the northwest side at the base of the shaft is a seated
male figure representing Law. He is dressed in classical
robes and in his proper left hand he holds a tablet.

So the formula for America's success—faith, morality, law,
education, and liberty—is represented in this monument. This
formula starts with faith. Our faith guides the development of an
internal morality of heart. This morality reveals itself as a standard
of good and bad. It is this standard of good and bad that results
in a moral system of law that enforces order and extends grace. It
is education that it supposed to teach these principles to future
generations so that we may continue to live in freedom.

This is the only recipe for freedom that has ever worked.
Not only has it worked, it has brought more joy, more prosperity,

and more generosity to more people than any other system of government in the history of the world.

We would do well to remember these principles. We would do well to go beyond remembering these principles and committing ourselves to once again embracing these principles, if not for ourselves then we should heed the words in the Preamble of our Constitution and seek to promote these principles for *our posterity*.

## WHAT SHOULD WE EXPECT OF OUR LEADERS?

*What are the most important attributes of leaders?*

Perhaps we should look for someone who passes the most bills. After all, some people see bill passage as a sign of effectiveness. On the other hand, if you believe in freedom and limited government, a large volume of bills resulting in a larger government may not be very appealing.

Perhaps we should be looking for the candidate that raises the most money. After all, if someone can raise a lot of money, it means that they know many successful and influential people that might have good ideas on how to make our citizens more successful. If someone raises the most money, then they can sponsor event after event so that people know that they truly care about their cause. On the other hand, someone who raises a lot of money often makes a lot of promises to his benefactors in return for those funds.

How about individuals who pass the most pieces of bi-partisan legislation? After all, if someone can pass bi-partisan legislation it might mean that the legislation has broad appeal to citizens. On the other hand, bi-partisan legislation may compromise timeless core principles that have been proven to work in favor of momentary political capital.

How about individuals who follow their party platform? After all, many voters vote straight ticket rather than evaluate the merits of each individual. It would be nice if voters could expect a high degree of consistency between the public service of an elected official and the party platform under which they were elected.

How about individuals who receive a desirable designation from third-party observers? For example, I have earned legislator of the year awards from the Police Officers Association, Senior Alliance, and Associated Builders and Contractors. Voters who value law enforcement, seniors, and businesses would tend to appreciate these designations. I have also earned the title of Most Conservative Senator multiple times. I would like to think that this designation would have merit in the eyes of many voters. After all, most Republicans run as conservatives during their campaigns because it appeals to the base. Even Democratic candidates typically moderate their rhetoric to some extent during campaigns to reflect conservative values. On the other hand, truly conservative principles are often at odds with the objectives of the Swamp.

How about electing a member of an experienced political family? Article I Section 9 of the US Constitution explicitly prohibits titles of nobility, but we do have modern day equivalents to aristocracy. How can you tell? Any time someone refers to a seat of elected office as the [Insert Name] seat instead of the people's seat, it is a good indicator. Families run generation after generation. Husbands are followed by wives. Brothers are followed by brothers. Name recognition is a powerful asset, but should our elected representatives be chosen primarily on the basis of name recognition?

As the former state chair of the Ted Cruz for President campaign in Michigan, I had the privilege of escorting Ted's dad, Rafael, to events across our state and listen to him speak. During his speeches, he invariably highlighted the importance of God's word when it comes to politics. In particular, he highlighted the importance of Exodus 18:21 as a guide for selecting political candidates: "But select capable men from all the people—men who fear God, trustworthy men who hate dishonest gain—and appoint them as officials over thousands, hundreds, fifties and tens." I agree.

Simply put, we should look for leaders that fear God, are trustworthy, and whose decisions are not influenced by bribes. This verse of Scripture serves as my guide for endorsing other candidates. Oh, and before some on the Left cite this as an example of a fictitious "war on women," let the record show that I have endorsed women as well as men. Let's look at each of these attributes a bit further.

*Why is the fear of God so important?* The reasons are laid out pretty clearly in the document that gave birth to our nation—the Declaration of Independence. According to this document signed by representatives from each of our original thirteen colonies, our rights have been endowed to us by our Creator. They were not granted to us by a king. Any leader who does not respect God does not respect the inalienable nature of our rights as Americans. If rights such as the right to life, liberty, and the pursuit of happiness are not inalienable, then we can be *alienated* from those rights by those who do not respect the source of those rights. Farfetched? One of the key tenets of Communism is the removal of God from the public square. In fact, Vladimir Lenin once remarked, "Atheism is a natural and inseparable part of Marxism, of the theory and practice of scientific socialism."[1] Communism is not exactly the poster child for life, liberty, and the pursuit of happiness.

Another reason that the fear of God is important is that people are flawed. As an elected official, whatever flaws you have are amplified under the microscope of a public campaign.

I once heard that John Adams observed that "the difference between a politician and a statesman is that politicians fear men while statesmen fear God." While I have not been able to confirm that John Adams is the original source of this observation, it does ring true. I believe that people are tired of politicians who shift positions based on the fear of public perception or the fear of colleagues. I believe our citizens are looking for statesmen.

*Why is being trustworthy so important?* In a republic, we elect people to be representatives of the public. Once elected, they become our representatives. As such, we need to be able to trust that their yes means yes and that their no means no. If they campaigned on a platform to protect life or Second Amendment rights, then you should be able to trust them to defend life and your Second Amendment rights. You shouldn't have to ask them for their position on issues they promoted during their campaign for office.

*What is not being subject to bribes so important?* It gets to the heart of whose voice is being listened to. Is it the voice of lobbyists or the voice of the people one was elected to represent?

I was on a flight seated next to a gentleman who was a long-time Democrat. When he found out that I was a Senator, he shared with me that he had actually voted for Donald Trump during this past election. When I asked why, he said that he felt taken for granted by the Democratic Party. As someone who started to become politically active as a member of a local Tea Party, I can assure you that there are many Republicans who feel the same way.

I believe that is why slogans such as Drain the Swamp and Make DC Listen resonated with so many voters this past election. It is also what is motivating so many voters to push for part-time legislators. On its face, it would seem that a part-time legislator would result in citizens having a part-time voice for them in DC or our state legislatures, but if one believes that their voice is already being ignored, what's the point of a full-time legislator?

It is important, therefore, to renew an appreciation for the term *servant* in the title of public servant. This goes well beyond the individual elected official. It is important for elected officials to hire office personnel who take the term *servant* seriously. It is important to staff an office with people who care about more than advancing the political ladder. That includes interns.

I am happy to say that I have been truly blessed to be surrounded by true public servants seeking the best interests of our constituents. I often receive compliments for my service that are a direct result of the actions taken by my team in Lansing. More often than not, it is my team who deserves all of the credit for this service.

The sad part is that we can't always help. Sometimes what people are asking for is not lawful or within our power to assist. Sometimes people attempt to use you or are looking for quid pro quo in return for assisting you in a campaign. In all such matters, it is important to stay true to the principles upon which you ran for office and took an oath to uphold.

Some other important attributes for any public official are accessibility and transparency. Along these lines, I believe it is reasonable to expect regular office hours held at reasonable times. I typically hold office hours twice a month—once around lunchtime in a senior center and another in the evening at libraries throughout my district.

In today's day and age, social media is an important and effective way to connect with constituents. I use Facebook and Twitter to provide daily updates to constituents on policy issues, explain controversial votes, and solicit feedback. I also put a lot of effort into maintaining my Senate office website at www. SenatorPatrickColbeck.com. The site includes a complete listing of our press releases, editorials, floor speeches, solutions, and much more.

My principled service to date has been appreciated by detractors as well as supporters. Here's a sample of what folks who would typically be detractors have said about me:

> The most reasonable thing about this bill was said by State Senator Patrick Colbeck of Canton, who is normally so far right he almost might be in a party by himself. But he does have principles. Colbeck voted no, saying "I'm tired of the businesses being prioritized over the best interest of everybody. There seems to be a push so that all the folks that are putting money into campaigns are the ones getting priority." What could be more shocking than a legislator who actually tells the truth?"
>
> —*Jack Lessenberry, newspaper columnist*

Thank you for supporting Michigan's public employees and the new solutions that we bring to the citizens of Michigan. Particularly for transparency.

*—BG, union representative*

Mind you they have also said many other things not suitable for print, but it is appreciated when they take the time to evaluate the substance of the service rather than stop at the party affiliation or other label.

Here's a sample of what some of my supporters have said about me:

Thanks for your efforts. You're the only one who has gotten anything done.

*— KG, union representative*

When I first came for my interview last December, I was surprised to see a few verses from the Bible on art on the walls of the office. I thought that was a great thing, but I did not realize then that I would see an office of politically involved people actually acting out their faith in an arena where it can be so difficult. The encouragement you guys have given me in standing up for what I believe is incredible. I have more confidence in my faith than ever before and from seeing the way you all place God at the center of your lives while still working in the government has given me so much assurance that I can do the same.

*—Allie, Senate Intern*

I wanted to personally thank you for your service to the
state. Your dedication to your constituents and your hard
work should make you and your family very proud!

—*SL, lobbyist*

Thank you for your commitment to integrity and your
desire for excellence in government. I appreciate all of your
hard work. Furthermore, I believe the work you are doing
will impact generations. Thank you all (Senator and Staff)
for being patriots!

—*RK, citizen*

I just wanted to write to you and give you thanks for the
kindness that you show my wife, at the Family Christian
Store in Canton. She works so hard and tries to be as
friendly and courteous as possible to all of her customers
but sometimes they can really be difficult and mean. . . .
However, every time you visit the store while she's working
she comes home and says that "her friend the Senator"
came in to the store today and it really lifts her spirits.
You're always so kind to her. She told me that over the
summer, during a really hot spell, you had been in the store
shopping and after you left you returned with cold bottles
of water for her and the other girl behind the counter. For
you I'm sure it seemed like such a small gesture but to
[my wife] it meant more than you can imagine. A State
Senator thinking about the well being of the minimum
wage girls behind the counter at the store. You represent
our state well. You represent Christians well. You represent
humanity well. There's no real reason behind the timing

of this email other than the fact that [my wife] and I were talking about the election last night and your name came up. She said she wishes that all of our politicians could be more like you!

—*CL, constituent*

Let's compare and contrast the comments from your esteemed colleagues from the 2nd and 14th districts – reading prepared remarks written who knows how long ago in obvious anticipation of the day. Remarks that were inflammatory at best and derogatory and divisive at worse, firing salvo after salvo of name calling and accusatory inference ("rabid ideologues" was my favorite) that accomplished nothing. Compare those to your obviously ad lib comments, not noticeable by their delivery but rather their timely, reflectivity comments of the events which just occurred. No finger pointing, name calling or adding fuel to the fire but rather offering an actual solution and goal that doesn't compound the problem in an effort to solve it. Kudos once again, sir. Your cool head and logical approach has no place in the Lansing of today, but hopefully will be the norm in the Lansing of tomorrow.

—*Facebook post*

On Wednesday, May 4, I was given the privilege to shadow state Sen. Patrick Colbeck. I got to sit in his three committee meetings and a legislative session. I got an inside view of how Lansing works. But I also got to see how great a person Sen. Colbeck truly is. I'm rather a cynic when it comes to politics, but I can say without a shadow of doubt that Colbeck is different from the typical connotations "politician" brings. His moral character, belief in our creator, his willingness to serve his district, and his friendly demeanor distinguish him as one with honorable character. So please don't lump Colbeck in with other politicians, even if his political views are the opposite of yours. I truly believe he is doing what he thinks is right, instead of what special interests think or what popular opinion is. I know—I campaigned for him, interviewed him, had lunch with him, I saw the way he conducted himself, and saw the questions and votes he did in committees and in session.

—*AM, constituent*

Feedback like the above helps to make the long hours, personal attacks, and difficult decisions seem worthwhile.

As a representative of more than 250,000 Michigan citizens, there is a certain amount of weight and prestige that goes with the title of Michigan state senator. If one does not enter the office with a certain degree of humility, one is not likely to find it while serving. The system is designed to place significant importance on those who serve that goes well beyond perfunctory titles like "honorable" and "senator." It truly is an honor to be elected by a majority of your constituents to represent them. Unfortunately, as Lord Acton wrote, "power tends to corrupt and absolute power corrupts absolutely." That holds true in the halls of capitols around our nation despite our noblest intentions. In fact, many of our representatives enter these positions of power and honor with the noblest of intentions, only to succumb to the influences of power brokers promising financial security and prestige. I am happy to say that I have been blessed to serve with many who have stayed true to the principles of duty and honor throughout their tenure of service. Regrettably, I have found this to be the exception and not the rule.

## WHAT CAN YOU DO?

We have all heard the term "silent majority." The fact is, we have not been all that silent over the past few years. We have spoken loudly at the ballot box. We may not hear our voices on the nightly news. We may not hear our voices in the stories and editorials found in newspapers. We do hear them, though.

I hear them on the way into church when someone stops to say "thank you for being our voice in Lansing". I hear them at the grocery store when someone stops to say "I follow you on Facebook. Thank you for keeping us informed". I hear them at office hours or when I knock on doors when people say "thank you for standing up for us". These singular voices of gratitude speak much louder at the ballot box than all of the acerbic "he said, she said" dialogue that passes for news nowadays.

What can you do? In short, be a good citizen. I explain what it means to be a good citizen in the next few pages.

### Reflect the Values You Seek

Our elected officials are not only called public servants. They are often also called representatives. This means that our elected officials often represent the values of those who elect them. If the voters are selfish and immoral, their representatives will be selfish and immoral. If the voters do not understand how our system of government is intended to operate, their representatives will not understand how our system of government is intended to operate. If the voters are not fiscally responsible, their representatives will not be fiscally responsible. If we wish our representatives in government to be good, we need to be good citizens.

### Know How the System Is Supposed to Work

In this book, I have done my best to help share some practical information related to how our government works, but it is no substitute for the two foundational social compacts of our nation: The Declaration of Independence and the US Constitution. All Americans should not only read but also study each of these documents.

It is never too late. In fact, sad as it may be, I did not read either of these documents from beginning to end until I was in my forties.

The Declaration of Independence defines our core values as Americans. The Constitution is not a long document. It is written plainly for all to understand. Our Founders wrote profusely on the Constitution most notably in the Federalist and Anti-Federalist papers.

If you are still looking for a better understanding, I recommend taking Hillsdale College's free ten-week online course on the Constitution or taking a Constitution Class from Rick Green of WallBuilders for an excellent primer. *The 5000 Year Leap* by Cleon Skousen should be required reading for all public school students.

### Seek the Truth

When Jesus stood before Pontius Pilate he testified that "You say that I am a king. In fact, the reason I was born and came into the world is to testify to the truth. Everyone on the side of truth listens to me" (John 18:37).

To which Pilate responded, "What is truth?"

In no other topic of discussion in our society is this question asked more than in discussions of politics. In fact, even the discussion between Jesus and Pilate dealt with politics.

The search for the truth is nothing new. Why is it so difficult to find? After all, we live in what some people refer to as the Information Age. We have access to more information than at any time in human history yet we still struggle to separate the proverbial wheat from the chaff in order to reveal the truth. Part of the problem is that there is a lot of chaff to sort through. We live in the era of fake news where news organizations protected under the First Amendment freedom of the press routinely abuse this protection to undermine the same system of government that secures this freedom.

The sad reality of life is that many of us don't really want to know the truth. In the words of Colonel Jessup, as played by Jack Nicholson in *A Few Good Men*, we "can't handle the truth." We prefer the comfort of our own worldview to the truth. Those who live in the comfort of their own worldview are the "kings" and "queens" of this world. The truth can be messy. It can create conflict. After all, Jesus was crucified for testifying to the truth.

So how do we seek the truth? Go to the source.

The media has considerable ability to prop someone up or tear them down. There is no substitute for going to the source whether that be a statement by an elected official or candidate. Context is important. For example, someone could accurately claim that the Bible says there is no God. However, the full passage in Psalms 14:1 says, "The fool says in his heart, 'There is no God.' " The full passage conveys a much different message, doesn't it? The same is true for excerpts from legislation or quotes from elected officials.

If the topic is a bill, read the bill. In Michigan, citizens can read the actual bill by going to http://legislature.mi.gov. Citizens can also review analyses provided by either the Senate or House Fiscal Agencies, which are known for being non-partisan. These are the same analyses that most legislators review. Please note that as bills are amended, sometimes there may be a lag between votes on the amended legislation and the posting of the amended version.

If the topic is a statement, read or listen to the actual words. We live in a world where almost everything is recorded for posterity. It is eerily similar to the world of George Orwell's *1984*. I have taken to recording most of my speaking engagements, including office hours, because political opponents have a propensity for taking clips out of context. We always need to have the complete statement available to provide full context.

If the topic is whether or not a given law is constitutional, read the law *and* the Constitution. The Supreme Court does not have a monopoly on discerning what is or is not constitutional. In fact, their presumed ability to rule on the constitutionality of a law is not even in the Constitution. They granted themselves this power via their *opinion* in *Marbury v Madison*. Congress didn't wish to create conflict so they did not assert their constitutional monopoly on legislative authority. The Supreme Court now routinely issues decisions that have assumed the force of law even if they override provisions in the U.S. Constitution or even state constitutions.

I realize that all of this truth seeking takes time. The most precious resource that many of us have is time. If you do not have time to seek the truth as outlined above, then I would recommend finding a trusted source from whom you can get the CliffNotes version of the truth. You will still need to invest some time up front validating your trusted source, but once validated, you will have a way to stay informed relatively easily. I recommend periodic fact checking just to make sure that your source stays on course. Journalists or citizen advocates, much like politicians, can stray off course if they start using the wrong compass.

### Share the Truth

Once you have identified the truth either through your own research or your very own "trusted source," it is important to share the truth. Remember, not everyone knows where to go for the truth. Be their trusted source. Don't abuse that trust.

How can you share the truth? We live in an age where individuals have an unprecedented ability to share information. The panoply of social media platforms alone enables one person to effectively become a news agency . . . for free. One can also be active with traditional media sources like newspapers by submitting letters to the editor.

As we seek to change the world through various media, though, don't neglect the home front. Our kids and grandkids need to hear the truth as well. Don't forget to use the kitchen table as a social media platform.

We also have a circle of friends with which we share meals and sometimes a round of golf. Don't be shy about sharing the truth with them as well. Sure, there are folks who attempt to make the topics of religion and politics taboo subjects, but *taboos* themselves are religious in nature. Keep in mind, those who would seek to undermine your faith and political views are not silent in their respective mediums. Pop culture openly mocks people of faith and increasingly pushes a leftist agenda. It is time to push back with the truth.

Our churches are supposed to be sources of truth in our society yet today even our churches avoid "taboo" subjects. In some respects, this is understandable. The church has been targeted by federal and state legislation designed to silence its voice. One of the most glaring examples of this legislation is the so-called Johnson Amendment. Paragraph 1 of Internal Revenue Code 7.25.3 describes organizations which may be exempt from US Federal income tax as follows:

> (3) Corporations, and any community chest, fund, or foundation, organized and operated exclusively for religious, charitable, scientific, testing for public safety, literary, or educational purposes, or to foster national or international amateur sports competition (but only if no part of its activities involve the provision of athletic facilities or equipment), or for the prevention of cruelty to children or animals, no part of the net earnings of which inures to the benefit of any private shareholder or individual, no substantial part of the activities of which is carrying on propaganda, or otherwise attempting, to influence legislation (except as otherwise provided in subsection (h)), and **which does not participate in, or intervene in (including the publishing or distributing of statements), any political campaign on behalf of (or in opposition to) any candidate for public office.[3]"**

The Johnson amendment is the bolded portion of this provision beginning with the words "which does not participate in." The amendment affects nonprofit organizations with 501(c)(3) tax exemptions, which are subject to absolute prohibitions on engaging in political activities and risk loss of tax-exempt status if violated.[2]

In response to the Johnson Amendment, in 2008 the Alliance Defending Freedom launched the Pulpit Initiative featuring Pulpit Freedom Sunday. What started with thirty-three pastors now features almost two thousand pastors. What is Pulpit Freedom Sunday?

> Pulpit Freedom Sunday is an event associated with the Pulpit Initiative, a legal effort designed to secure the free speech rights of pastors in the pulpit. Pulpit Freedom Sunday encourages pastors to exercise their constitutionally protected freedom to speak truth into every area of life from the pulpit. Alliance Defending Freedom also hopes to eventually go to court to have the Johnson Amendment struck down as unconstitutional for its regulation of sermons, which are protected by the First Amendment.[3]

The IRS refuses to enforce the Johnson Amendment because doing so would trigger a lawsuit which they would lose. You see, the IRS would prefer that pastors live in fear. The Bible says "Do not be afraid" sixty-three times. It is critical that our pulpits cast aside fear and share the truth.

In Michigan, there is actually a law on the books that targets individual clergy not simply religious organizations. Religious leaders are the only people singled out under state law (MCL

168.931) for speaking out on election-related topics, meaning they can go to jail for saying things everyone else can say without consequence. Under this law, religious leaders are guilty of a misdemeanor subject to a five hundred dollar fine and/or ninety days in jail for such actions.

The current law has been challenged in the past by a good friend of mine, Dr. Levon Yuille, pastor of the Bible Church in Ypsilanti. Pastor Yuille is also the national director of the National Black Pro-Life Congress and the former chairman of the Michigan Black Republican Council of Southern Michigan. In 2012, the American Freedom Law Center (AFLC) filed a federal civil rights lawsuit in the US District Court in Detroit, challenging this provision of Michigan's election law and asking for an injunction to be issued on the law. The Sixth Circuit denied AFLC's petition requesting a full court review.

I find it shameful that religious leaders have been singled out for such prohibitions. The so-called separation of church and state philosophy President Thomas Jefferson referenced in his letter to the Danbury Baptist church was intended to protect churches from the state, not muzzle their right to free speech. Clergy are not passing laws "respecting the establishment" of any specific religion. What is at issue is the clear attempt by the state to "restrict the free exercise thereof."

You don't have to be a pastor to share the truth. There are other ways to share the truth that revolve around the everyday activities of life. You can share the truth while waiting to pick up your kids at school or at PTA meetings. You can share the truth at the barbershop or grocery store. You can share the truth in community organizations, such as Kiwanis, Rotary, Lions Club, or Shriners. Anywhere you go is a prime opportunity to share the truth. Despite what some would have you believe, there is no mention of a "free speech zone" in the Constitution.

### Become a Policy Advocate

Once you have sought the truth and have been actively sharing the truth within your circle of influence, it is natural and commendable to reach out to your elected officials directly and become a policy advocate. One can do this as an individual or as a member of a larger organization that you either create or join. Another term for policy advocate is *lobbyist*.

Advocacy can be as simple as expressing support or opposition for a given piece of legislation in a phone call, email, letter, or visit with a legislator. It can also involve organizing protests, forming political action committees (PACs), or launching petition drives. The most effective policy advocacy efforts are those that combine financial and election-related incentives or those that have become trusted sources of good policy information for legislators. Unions are prime examples of policy advocacy organizations that combine financial contributions with a large voter base in support of their policy influencing efforts. State policy network organizations such as the Mackinac Center or the Citizens Research Council are examples of trusted sources of good policy information for legislators.

The sheer variety of policy issues dictates that it is virtually impossible for any legislator to be an expert on all of the policy issues on which they are expected to vote. In light of this, it is easy to see why most responsible legislators seek out subject matter experts whom they can trust. These experts might be trusted friends, fellow legislators, staff members, or even lobbyists.

Trust is extremely important in politics. Trust is often what drives voters to vote for a given candidate. Trust is also often the main consideration for an elected official when considering voting yes or no on a bill. It is often very difficult, even upon reading a bill, to discern the potential impacts of the legislation with any degree of certainty. Bad votes are matters of public record for eternity. One really bad vote can trump hundreds of good votes in the career of an elected official. What makes the job of legislator extremely difficult is that a "bad" vote does not always correlate to what was actually voted upon. It correlates with public perception of what is voted upon. The more citizens we have seeking the truth, the less of a gap there is between public perception and the truth.

One's reputation is extremely important in politics. A political official's name is a brand much like Coca Cola or Ford. A good brand image with voters leads to election success. A bad brand image with voters can lead to much disappointment. Knowing this, some policy advocates seek to influence legislators via smear campaigns. These advocates take advantage of the fact that politicians are some of the least trusted people in America because they often push narratives that contradict the truth. Granted, there are many politicians in the "Swamp" who should be held accountable for their actions, but what happens when you set out to smear one that is actually telling the truth?

As a legislator, I have experienced good advocacy and bad advocacy. Much like in Charles Dickens beloved novel *A Tale of Two Cities*, I have experienced the best of times and I have experienced the worst of times when it comes to interacting with policy advocates. As I've mentioned earlier, good policy advocates are all about pursuing and sharing the truth. I may disagree with their policy views, but I respect their advocacy efforts when they are rooted in a pursuit of the truth. Not all advocates are interested in the truth, however. Some are simply interested in power.

The corrupting influence of power is not limited to those who seek elected office. In fact, some people prefer to destroy others in political office rather than run for office and subject themselves to the same level of scrutiny as the candidates they are trying to bring down. Sadly, there are people who actually enjoy destroying the reputations of others even to the point of lying. One glaring example of this approach to policy advocacy was a group of people who share the same policy goal that I do—the elimination of Common Core Standards in Michigan. Much like many elected officials, they started out on the right track. They established a solid reputation for seeking the truth and sharing the truth with others. They then turned to organized policy advocacy. In this role, they drafted their own legislation to repeal the Common Core Standards in Michigan, which I introduced in the Senate and another legislator introduced in the House.

While deliberations stalled in the House, as a member of the Senate Education Policy, I was able to get a hearing and a favorable report of my bill onto the Senate floor. That is where I hit a roadblock. You may recall that the Senate Majority Leader and I did not see eye to eye on the need to repeal Common Core Standards. So in order to reach the important 56-20-1 threshold, I came up with some changes that would be needed to pass the legislation. No changes were required to earn my support for the bill. After all, I introduced it and voted in favor of it in the Senate Education Policy Committee. Changes were required to get to 56-20-1, however. I made sure that these changes did not violate the end game of repealing Common Core standards and replace them with the pre-Common Core Massachusetts standards. I approached the advocacy group that drafted the original legislation regarding these changes. Their leader emailed me saying they would rather have no bill pass then one that had been changed.

It all came down to trust. I was, and still am, committed to repealing Common Core standards, but their model bill contained many provisions besides the repeal of Common Core that guaranteed the bill wouldn't pass. If the repeal of Common Core were our true goal, the rest of the provisions needed to be negotiable. These advocates had witnessed other states watered down repeal legislation that resulted in no true repeal at all. They were concerned that *any* changes to their version of the legislation would be another fake repeal bill. When I persisted in my proposal to retain the repeal language and remove references to provisions that were of concern to the Senate Majority Leader and governor, they began labeling my legislation as a fake repeal bill. In other words, they labeled their staunchest policy advocate as an opponent.

It didn't stop at accusations of a fake repeal bill. They launched a campaign of personal destruction. They used their reputation as subject matter experts on Common Core Standards and the general perception of all politicians as liars to push a "my way or the highway" approach to policy advocacy. They used social media and events across the state to impugn my integrity by publicizing incomplete information about me that painted a false picture. It didn't work. Despite a plethora of resolutions and platform provisions, Michigan still has Common Core Standards all because this policy advocacy group made the issue radioactive by attacking the motivations of their lead supporter in the Senate.

There is no better way to become ineffective at policy advocacy than to spread false information or promote innuendo as fact. Trust is everything in the realm of politics. Our Constitution is often referred to as a social compact. It is a formal acknowledgment that we the people have entrusted elected officials with a finite amount of political power to be used in the best interest of our general welfare. Therefore, attempts to undermine this trust by promoting false information not only undermines policy advocacy efforts, it undermines our system of government.

If your passion for policy advocacy is specific to a given political party's platform, you may wish to serve on party committees. Party committees are often organized by congressional district and county. Election to these local party committees can lead to elections to the state committee or even the national committee. One can also donate one's time in support of party policies as a precinct delegate. In Michigan, precinct delegates are elected positions, and their core responsibility is to understand the key issues and sentiments of party voters within their voting precinct. In this capacity, they are invaluable resources to party candidates in the general election. Precinct delegates in Michigan also play pivotal roles in committee elections that occur during county, state, and national conventions. In Michigan, precinct delegates vote to elect the candidates for the lieutenant governor, attorney general, secretary of state, public university boards, state board of education, and the Supreme Court.

If you seek to become a policy advocate, please make the pursuit of truth the foundation of your advocacy. I have found that this foundation can be used as a catalyst to enable the discussion of common policy objectives. Once you have common policy objectives, it is then fairly straightforward to achieve 56-20-1.

### *Run for Office*

After leaving office in 1909, Theodore Roosevelt went on a speaking tour and on April 23, 1910, gave a resounding speech, "The Man in the Arena" at the Sorbonne in Paris. In the speech he said:

> It is not the critic who counts; not the man who points out how the strong man stumbles, or where the doer of deeds could have done them better. The credit belongs to the man who is actually in the arena, whose face is marred by dust and sweat and blood; who strives valiantly; who errs, who comes short again and again, because there is no effort without error and shortcoming; but who does actually strive to do the deeds; who knows great enthusiasms, the great devotions; who spends himself in a worthy cause; who at the best knows in the end the triumph of high achievement, and who at the worst, if he fails, at least fails while daring greatly, so that his place shall never be with those cold and timid souls who neither know victory nor defeat.

I have done my best in this book to give you an inside peek into how our political system works, but there is no better way to gain an appreciation for the challenges of public service than to run for office yourself.

Before doing so, though, I strongly recommend immersing yourself in fervent prayer. Before you run, be honest with yourself and make sure you

- Know why,
- Know what,

- Know how, and
- Know who.

*Know why.* Knowing why you want to run for office will help to guide your actions—not just in the campaign but during your service should you win your election. From my experience, there are five basic reasons why someone would run for office: need a job, family tradition, party loyalty, resolve a specific policy issue, or answer a call of faith. These reasons revolve around who or what you are seeking to serve. Do you seek to serve your own best interests? Perhaps you need a job or see the position as a stepping stone to bigger and better personal opportunities. Do you seek to serve the best interests of a group of friends or colleagues? Perhaps your family has always run for office and you are being encouraged to continue the family tradition or perhaps you have established relationships with certain individuals whom you would like to see succeed. Do you seek to serve a set of party principles? Perhaps you believe in the principles espoused by a given political party or movement and would like to see them driving government policies. Do you seek to serve the best interests of all of the people? Perhaps you are focused upon the oath of office that you take and seek to support the principles embedded within our Constitution.

*Know what.* Knowing what you want to do once in office is typically expressed as your "platform." Your platform will take center stage in your campaign materials, stump speeches, and website. Your platform will also help you discern what committees you should seek in order to enact the planks in your platform. You should have a good understanding of these committees well before your election as leadership candidates will be asking for your support throughout your campaign. Committee assignments can be used as bargaining chips in leadership elections.

*Know how.* It is my intent that this book will provide you with an effective starting point on this topic, but I do recommend hiring a campaign consultant to help take you across the finish line.

*Know who.* Nobody wins elections or leads by themselves. It is important to know who to align with and who not to align with early on. Much like on the reality show *Survivor*, in politics you must be careful with whom you align. Friends can be temporary, but enemies often last a very long time.

I have no way of guaranteeing your victory in this pursuit, but one thing I will guarantee. If you decide to run for office: it will change your life.

### Support Those Who Run for Office

If you want to have good representation in government, it is important to support good people who run for office. It is not enough to sit in the bleachers and wish them well. You need to support them on the field of battle—not just during an election but also during their time in office. Remember, there are plenty of other voices for them to listen to. And most of the voices politicians hear are those who are paid by special interest groups to make sure they are heard. It is imperative upon you to be someone they know will have their back when the going gets tough—and if they are doing anything worth doing, it will get tough.

Support for those who run for office can take many forms. Supporting a candidate with your vote is the most obvious and important way, but there are quite a few other ways to show support. You can offer financial support. That is how influential donors and special interest groups demonstrate support for a given candidate. If you are not a person of significant financial means, don't be discouraged from making a small donation in support of a true public servant. Ten thousand $10 donations equals ten $10,000 donations, and ten thousand $10 donations correlate to ten thousand votes. Donations may win headlines, but votes win elections.

Another important way to support a candidate is with your time. Every campaign needs volunteers, but please don't limit your volunteering just to election season. I for one have been blessed with a great group of supporters who lend their support during office hours, along parade routes, or by sending letters to the editor. Support throughout the term helps legislators retain the courage to tackle politically difficult issues.

If you are someone with prominent name recognition in the community, you may want to consider issuing a formal endorsement of your preferred candidate. Whenever I am asked for an endorsement, I evaluate the candidate in context of Exodus 18:21. It is my hope that you would use these same guidelines when you choose whom to support.

Another vital component in the discussion of supporting those who run for office is expectation management. It is easy to get emotionally invested in our preferred candidate, especially in the middle of a heated election. When we find someone who professes the same positions on the issues that mean a lot to us, it is easy to put our candidate on a pedestal. We tend to forget that elected officials are still people, and people are not perfect. We have all supported candidates who have let us down. When was the last time you agreed with someone 100 percent of the time? Should we stop supporting someone just because they differed with your view on a given issue? Have you ever found yourself reconsidering your position on a given issue? Sometimes a candidate may have received more information about a policy issue that caused them to change their mind. And sometimes God might be doing a mighty work with an imperfect politician, and He may use your support to accomplish such a work.

### Focus Upon What Is Noble and True

We live in an imperfect world. That is one of the side effects of living in a world filled with imperfect people. That doesn't mean that we shouldn't strive to look beyond these imperfections and focus upon what is noble, excellent, and praiseworthy as spelled out in Philippians 4:8.

It can be tempting to focus upon our imperfections. Such a focus can be very divisive. If left unchecked, this divisiveness can undermine our system of government. Our nation is called the *United* States of America, yet we don't seem to be very united nowadays. As a matter of fact, we seem to be quite divided.

Why are we divided? I don't profess to have a comprehensive answer to that question, but I believe that one of the clues that may lead us to such an answer surfaced at a community meeting that I attended in Detroit. The state's School Reform Office had recently chosen to close thirty-eight underperforming schools, and the Senate Education Policy Committee had been conducting a series of hearings regarding how best to hold schools accountable. Three of the proposed school closings impacted families in attendance at the community meeting. They did not want the schools to be closed. I didn't want the schools to be closed. Based upon the comments from the community, it was obvious that the closure of these schools would have created an effective education "desert" in the community. Seeing an issue from the perspective of the people impacted is an important first step in resolving any issue, so I went to the event in order to better understand how the school closings would impact the community.

The organizer for the event pitched a methodology he referred to as Restorative Practices as a formula for conflict resolution. On its surface, it did seem to promote some practices that would encourage people to view situations from another person's perspective. As I listened to the facilitator walk people through the Restorative Practices methodology, however, it became evident to me that there was a fatal flaw in the framework. Rather than bring people closer together, it seemed to open old wounds. Listening to the attendees, there seemed to be no shortage of people who had been offended by someone or some group. It created an environment that encouraged a seemingly endless stream of cries of injustice. These cries led to inevitable calls for restorative justice where the offender makes amends to the one offended.

When it was my turn to share all of the times that I had been wronged, I said something that probably seemed a bit strange. I shared that I have indeed been subject to many injustices, but I said that I chose rather to focus upon what is noble, true, excellent, and praiseworthy. It is easy to be offended. It can be much more difficult to overlook an offense. For some people, it may seem impossible. With Christ, though, nothing is impossible (see Phil 4:13). Not only is it possible, it is expected of those who profess to follow Jesus. That is what Christ asks us to do. He set the example in that while we were still sinners, Christ gave His life for ours. That is a different standard from the standard promoted by the world and is a standard that yields unity.

Have I always lived up to this standard? Regrettably, no, but I keep pressing on nonetheless. Whenever I have lived up to this standard, I have been able to accomplish amazing things like helping to make Michigan a Right to Work state. Sometimes, even my most ardent antagonists have taken notice.

The bottom line is that if you are looking to be offended, you will be offended. The important thing in life is how one reacts to such offenses. In fact, a key tenet of the Saul Alinksy tactics taught by progressives is that the "action is in the reaction." A common tactic is to poke and prod the subject of their animosity until the subject reacts in a way that they can exploit. More often than not, I simply choose to shake the dust off my feet and move on. Much to my opponent's consternation, I sleep well at night.

There is much that is noble, much that is excellent, and much that is praiseworthy in this world. It is my hope that this book will equip you with insights that will equip you to shape the policies in a way that are truly noble, excellent, and praiseworthy.

# 15

# THE FOUND DECADE

I have explained how Michigan had a Lost Decade—the first ten years of the millennium when Michigan lost jobs and citizens. Nearly a decade later, I believe it is safe to say that we are well on our way to finding our groove once again. In fact, I believe it is safe to say that we in Michigan are in the early stages of the "Found Decade."

Our population is growing again. It is easy to see why.

Business climate has surged from forty-ninth to eleventh.

Michigan is number 1 in the country for the creation of manufacturing jobs.

Michigan is number 1 in the Midwest for job creation.

Over 470,000 new private sector jobs have been created.[1]

I am happy to report that as of April 2017, Michigan had an unemployment rate of 5.4 percent, twenty-fifth in the nation. One of our biggest challenges now is finding qualified employees to fill our job vacancies. Within a thirty-mile radius of my Senate district alone there are over thirty-one thousand job openings.

It wasn't until 2012 that a strong rebound in private-sector employment materialized. Michigan passed our Right to Work law on December 12, 2012. The law prohibits employers from making an employee financially support a union as a condition of employment. One slogan repeated by union advocates then was that the new law was "right-to-work-for-less."[2] In the wake of the passage of Right to Work, Michigan is now number 4 in the nation for per capita income growth. In 2009, at the low point of the Michigan's Lost Decade, residents of thirty-nine other states had a higher income than people in Michigan did. We have risen to number 31 on this critical measure of economic health. In fact, Michigan's per capita personal income grew faster than that of forty other states in 2016. Regionally, only Indiana saw incomes rise faster. Indiana adopted Right to Work a year before Michigan.

Clearly, Michigan is now once again on the right track economically.

The Found Decade is not simply about facts and figures, though. It is about keeping families together. It is about encouragement. It is about hope.

All of these improvements should not come as a surprise to fans of the movie *Facing the Giants*. One of my favorite lines from the movie is "Is there anything that God cannot do?" Clearly for us, the answer has been unequivocally No.

# EPILOGUE

It is my hope that this book has provided some valuable insights on what it means to get into the wheelbarrow.

How has our life changed?

My wife put it this way. She used to get the paper and look at the travel section. She now looks at the front page and political section. I used to look at the sports and comics sections. Now they are the first sections jettisoned to the recycle bin. We used to travel quite a bit on vacation. We now enjoy "staycations." Since being together at home happens so rarely, it has become a novelty—plus it is less expensive. I used to enjoy playing golf, volleyball, and basketball. I now hit the elliptical as I watch TV to catch the news of the day or watch a documentary related to a public policy issue.

From a worldly perspective, much has changed—and not much of it has been for the better. From a spiritual perspective, however, much has changed—and it has *all* been for the better.

Our faith in God has grown immeasurably. We have found that the more we rely on Him, the more He sustains us. Throughout the journey in the wheelbarrow, God has *never* let us down.

Along the way, we have learned a lot about how our government really works.

We have learned a lot about why our government sometimes does not seem to work well. We have learned a lot about why many people have lost trust in our government. We have also learned a lot about how people can restore their trust in our government. Throughout the entire journey, we have learned the importance of faith.

Not faith in oneself.

Not faith in any person.

Not faith in any political party.

Not even faith in our precious piece of parchment known as our Constitution.

No, I am talking about the importance of faith in the God who knits all of these together into a truly exceptional system of governance that is uniquely American.

We have learned a lot about our own personal faith in God. We found that it is one thing to "talk the talk" about being a Christian. It is quite another to "walk the walk" and put that faith in action.

You may recall when the people of Israel first crossed the Jordan River that the water did not stop flowing until the priests stepped into the water. Stepping into the water was an act of faith for the Israelites as much as stepping into the wheelbarrow was for Angie and me.

This faith journey has not been easy. Not because God doesn't want us to enjoy the wheelbarrow ride, but because we have a tendency to try to get out and steer. For example, when it comes to finances, we learned that we prefer silos but God prefers manna. A word of advice, keep your hands and feet in the ride at all times. He will provide you with your daily bread if you put your faith fully in Him.

Along the way, God has enriched our lives with friendships well beyond our limited circle before running for office. We have met with prominent elected officials across the nation. We have met celebrities. We have met lonely people in need of knowing that they are not alone. We have met fellow Christians praying for us. We have met with truly honorable men and women in our armed forces and law enforcement communities. We have met teachers fighting the good fight of faith in our public schools where the views of Christian conservatives are not always welcome. We have met pastors seeking to awaken their flock to the need not only to speak out but to do so in love. We have met some truly remarkable men and women of faith who have encouraged us through prayer, kind words, and even sacrificial financial support.

We believe that God has used us to help change the political environment in Michigan in concert with others—even those who don't support this mission.

Our wheelbarrow ride is not over. The next leg in our journey to clean up government is to run for Governor of Michigan. If you are reading this book after November 6, 2018, you will know how far this latest journey has gone. We are comforted in the knowledge that our final destination is for God to determine not us.

Getting into the wheelbarrow may have been a scary decision at first, but it was also the best decision that we ever made. This world needs more wheelbarrow riders.

If Jesus asks, it is my hope that you will join Angie and me by getting into the wheelbarrow!

# NOTES

## PROLOGUE

1. The story is derived from the reportedly true story about a famous French tightrope walker from the 1860s named Charles Blondin.

## CHAPTER 1: THE LOST DECADE

1. Business Leaders for Michigan, "Michigan Turnaround Plan," June 2010, https://businessleadersformichigan.com/wp-content/uploads/2011/01/Business-Leaders-2011-MTP-Status-Report.pdf.

2. "Sure Glad That Decade is over!" *Data Driven Detroit* blog, January 2011, http://datadrivendetroit.org/2011/01/.

3. Tom Gantert, "Michigan's 'Lost Decade' Was Historic," Michigan Capitol Confidential, October 6, 2014, http://www.michigancapitolconfidential.com/20563.

4. "Databases, Tables & Calculators by Subject," Bureau of Labor Statistics, http://data.bls.gov/timeseries/LASST260000000000003?data_tool=XGtable.

5. "Unemployment Rates for States Annual Average Rankings 2010 - Present," Rhode Island Department of Labor and Training, http://www.dlt.ri.gov/lmi/laus/us/annavg.htm.

6. Business Leaders for Michigan, "Michigan Turnaround Plan," June 2010, https://businessleadersformichigan.com/wp-content/uploads/2011/01/Business-Leaders-2011-MTP-Status-Report.pdf.

## CHAPTER 5: HOW MICHIGAN BECAME A RIGHT-TO-WORK STATE

1. The law actually took effect on March 23, 2013 due to lack of immediate effect. When immediate effect is not granted, a law does not take effect until ninety days after sine die (literally, without a day).

2. John J. Miller, "How right-to-work won in Michigan," *National Review*, December 31, 2012, https://www.nationalreview.com/nrd/articles/336194/new-wisconsin.

3. "Unemployment Rates for States Annual Average Rankings 2010 - Present," Rhode Island Department of Labor and Training, http://www.dlt.ri.gov/lmi/laus/us/annavg.htm.

4. Jarrett Skorup, "Income Growth In Right-to-Work States Significantly Higher," Capcon blog, June 5, 2014, http://www.michigancapitolconfidential.com/income-growth-in-right-to-work-states-higher.

5. SOURCE: Bureau of Labor Statistics

## CHAPTER 6: PROTECTING OUR RIGHTS

1. If you doubt that there is a war against religion, I encourage you to read the Family Research Council's "Hostility to Religion" report found here: http://www.frc.org/hostilityreport.

## CHAPTER 7: LEADING WITHOUT LEGISLATION

1. More information available at http://www.senatorpatrickcolbeck.com/education/.

## CHAPTER 11: WHAT HAPPENS WHEN ONE UPSETS THE "SWAMP"?

1. Megan Wells, "The FBI's 10 Most Dangerous Cities," EfficientGov, February 2, 2017, https://efficientgov.com/blog/2017/02/02/fbi-10-dangerous-cities/.

2.   William H. Schmidt, Richard T. Houang, "Curricular Coherence and the Common Core State Standards for Mathematics," Michigan State University, November 1, 2012, http://journals. sagepub.com/doi/abs/10.3102/0013189X12464517.

## CHAPTER 12: IMPORTANT GOVERNANCE PRINCIPLES

1.   Brown Magic, "Peter's Laws for the Sociopathic Obsessive Compulsive Entrepreneur," Bling blog, September 25, 2005, http://theo-s.blogspot.com/2005/09/peters-laws-for-sociopathic-obsessive.html.

2.   I have subsequently learned that it was Milton Friedman who first expressed this framework.

3.   Adam Smith, *The Theory on Moral Sentiments* (Edinburg: Alexander Kincaid and J. Bell, 1759), emphasis added.

4.   Ibid.

5.   Alexis de Tocqueville, *Democracy in America* (New York: J. & H. G. Langley, 1841), 337.

6.   Ibid, 334.

7.   Ibid, 336.

8.   Ibid, 345.

9.   Ibid, 335.

10.  Attributed to Alexis de Tocqueville by Dwight D. Eisenhower in his final campaign address in Boston, Massachusetts, November 3, 1952, http://www.bartleby.com/73/829.html.

## CHAPTER 13: BOLD-COLORED SOLUTIONS

1.   Katie Bo Williams, "The 16 most absurd ICD-10 codes," HealthcareDive, August 15, 2015, http://www.healthcaredive. com/news/the-16-most-absurd-icd-10-codes/285737/.

2.   Avik Roy, "Why the American Medical Association Had 72 Million Reasons to Shrink Doctors' Pay," Forbes, November 28, 2011, https://www.forbes.com/sites/theapothecary/2011/11/28/ why-the-american-medical-association-had-72-million-reasons-to-help-shrink-doctors-pay/#4d700fc060d9.

3.  Qliance Medical Management Inc., "Primary Care Model Delivers 20 Percent Lower Overall Healthcare Costs, Increases Patient Satisfaction," January 15, 2015, http://www.senatorpatrickcolbeck.com/wp-content/uploads/2013/11/Qliance-study-shows-monthly-savings.pdf.

4.  Author interview with Dr. Josh Umbehr, AtlasMD, fall 2013.

5.  Databases, Tables & Calculators by Subject, Bureau of Labor Statistics, accessed December 2017, https://data.bls.gov/timeseries/LASST26000000000000004?amp percent253bdata_tool=XGtable&output_view=data&include_graphs=true.

6.  Bob Graves, "Power Plays: The Increasingly Competitive Electricity Landscape," Governing blog, September 23, 2015, http://www.governing.com/blogs/view/gov-local-government-electricity-competition-monopoly-challenge.html.

7.  According to the Bureau of Labor Statistics, Michigan has added 475,000 net new jobs since 2011. The August 2016 unemployment rate was at 4.5 percent.

8.  $0.16/kW-Hr, 6800 kW for Ann Arbor Data Center results in $1,008/hr results in $9.5M/yr for electricity.

9.  2016 testimony by school superintendents before legislative committees stated that their participation in the electric choice programs in Michigan saved them 20 percent per year.

10. Typically, there are six technicians plus one general manager per data center. Eleven million dollars in credits apply to four hundred employees, which correlates to fifty-seven data centers. Fifty-seven data centers times $950,000 savings per center equals $54.5 million in savings.

11. Average of $1,270 per year on electricity for Michigan residents

12. Based on $18,142 per year for average family assuming 100 percent employer coverage.

13. A minimum of four hundred jobs at $18,142 per year for health care correlates to $7.3 million per year. A 20 percent savings yields $1.4 million in savings.

14. "Health Insurance: Premiums and Increases," National Conference of State Legislatures, December 4, 2017, http://www.ncsl.org/research/health/health-insurance-premiums.aspx.

15. John F. Kennedy Moon Speech - Rice Stadium, September 12, 1962. https://er.jsc.nasa.gov/seh/ricetalk.htm.

16. John Wisely and JC Reindl, "Detroit's election woes: 782 more votes than voters," *Detroit Free Press*, December 18, 2016, http://www.freep.com/story/news/local/michigan/detroit/2016/12/18/detroit-ballots-vote-recount-election-stein/95570866/.

17. "Fast Facts 2018," Michigan Department of Transportation, https://www.michigan.gov/documents/mdot/MDOT_fastfacts02-2011_345554_7.pdf

18. Ibid.

19. Based upon data provided by MDOT that indicates that 1844 trunkline lane-miles go from Fair to Poor each year at current funding levels.

## CHAPTER 14: RESTORING FAITH IN GOVERNMENT

1. V. I. Lenin, Religion, (New York: International Publishers, 1933), 5, http://ciml.250x.com/archive/lenin/english/lenin_religion.pdf.

2. United States Internal Revenue Service.gov, https://www.irs.gov/irm/part7/irm_07-025-003.

3. Christiana Holcomb, "Pulpit Initiative | Pulpit Freedom Sunday," Alliance Defending Freedom, December 13, 2017, http://www.adfmedia.org/news/prdetail/4360.

## CHAPTER 15: THE FOUND DECADE

1. "Databases, Tables & Calculators by Subject," Bureau of Labor Statistics, https://data.bls.gov/timeseries/LASST260000000000005?amp percent253bdata_tool=XGtable&output_view=data&include_graphs=true.

2. "Michigan Incomes Up Strong After 4 Years of 'Right-to-Work-for-Less'," For the Record blog, April 3, 2017, http://www.michigancapitolconfidential.com/michigan-incomes-up-strong-after-4-years-of-right-to-work-for-less.

# ABOUT THE AUTHOR

With over two decades of private sector experience and two terms in the Michigan Senate, Patrick Colbeck distinguishes himself from career politicians and newcomers yet to navigate the troubled waters of Lansing. He has a track record of taking on big challenges and succeeding. He applied his degrees in Aerospace Engineering from the University of Michigan to design systems as an engineer with Boeing that enable human beings to live in space. He challenged our youth to dream big as an instructor at Space Camp. He knows what it's like for small business owners to take a leap of faith and setup shop. After six years of running his own small business, he sought to fix our state by running for the Michigan Senate. In his successful Senate bid, Colbeck became the first person elected directly into the Michigan Senate in over three decades without any political experience—and he defeated four former state representatives in the process. In the crucible of public service, he has remained true to the principles which he promised voters to uphold. He has been recognized as the most conservative senator the past two years in a row and three times in his seven years of service. He led the Senate effort to turn around Michigan's economy by restoring the freedom of assembly to rank and file workers and making Michigan the twenty-fourth Right-to-Work state in the nation. In recognition of his leadership role, he received the Senator Paul Fannin Statesman of the Year Award. His free market health care solutions that lower costs and improve services are nationally recognized and featured by Forbes. He has also been honored as the legislator of the year by the Police Officers Association of Michigan, the Senior Alliance, and Associated Builders and Contractors. His service goes well beyond legislative duties. In 2011, he co-founded the Michigan Freedom Center whose mission is "Serving those who serve us" in the military. Senator Colbeck also is a 2018 candidate to be Michigan's next governor. His integrity and principled service have been recognized by both his supporters and his detractors. In the final analysis, the senator has a proven record of bold solutions that prioritize the best interests of the citizens of Michigan above his own personal best interests. Patrick has been married to his college sweetheart, Angie, for 22 years.

95674812R00190

Made in the USA
Columbia, SC
20 May 2018